F

MW01138332

Excerpts selected, adapted and commented
from "The Spirits' Book," of Allan Kardec

Laura Bergallo

*Collaboration and translation from the Original French of
"Le Livre des Spirits"*
Gilberto Perez Cardoso

Translated to English by the Spiritist Alliance for Books, Inc.

Original Title: O Livrinho dos Espíritos (2002) – Ler Bem Editora - Rio de Janeiro - Brazil

Main entry under title:
THE LITTLE SPIRITS' BOOK For Young Adults and Beginners

1. Religious Philosophy 2. Spiritist Doctrine 3. Christianity

Translated by SAB's Team: Jussara Korngold, Monica Santos Lorena Suppa, Fred Lima and Danny Claudio
Final Editing: Gabriel Korngold and Nancy Hoppe
Cover Drawing and Design: Glaucia de Barros

Edited and revised by the Editorial and Publishing Department of the Spiritist Group of New York (SGNY) and the Spiritist Alliance for Books (SAB) 2010.

The Spiritist Alliance for Books (SAB) is a non-profit organization, which has the sole aim to promote and disseminate the Spiritist Doctrine in English, as codified by Allan Kardec.
SAB was officially established on April 12th, 2001. However, some of its participants have been earnestly fostering the dissemination of Spiritism in the United States and in the United Kingdom for over sixteen years.
The Spiritist Alliance for Books (SAB) is an organization that aims to unite people from all over the world who are willing to volunteer in the effort of translating spiritist books (which were originally written in other languages) into English.

"Blessed are the pure in heart, for they will see God."
    Jesus
(Matthew, 5: 8)

To **Allan Kardec**, *the Codifier of Spiritism, with deep respect and gratitude for the light that he brought to the world.*

Table of Contents

Preface to the English Edition

The Spirit's Book by Allan Kardec defined and served as the foundation for all Spiritist Literature to come. Over the years, the knowledge imparted in this book enriched my life in ways I cannot describe. As a natural consequence and, most importantly as a mother, I envisioned the impact a version of this book, primed specially for young people, would have. As a practicing Spiritist, I would like nothing better than to provide children with an opportunity to benefit from its wealth of knowledge and inspiration as I did.

Understandably, the effort to convert the language to simpler terms could not be an easy task. We are all indebted to Ms. Bergallo for accepting the challenge. In the book's introduction she gives insights into the difficulties she encountered. We can see that her experience in writing for children and adolescents served her well during this enterprise.

I asked my teenage son to proofread the book and waited impatiently for his comments. After years of attending services at a Spiritist Center and particularly doctrinal instructions in children and youth groups he is, at this time, ready for more mature Spiritual matters. His comment was remarkably gratifying: "Mom, now I understand what is written in this book."

Can you imagine my happiness when I heard that? It is my sincere hope that this version brings to parents in all English-speaking countries the same joy and fulfillment that it has brought my family.

Jussara Korngold,

Spiritist Group of New York, Inc. - Founder and President
Spiritist Alliance for Books, Inc. - Founder and President

New York, January 2010

Allan Kardec and "The Spirits' Book"

Hippolyte Léon Denizard Rivail, known throughout the world as Allan Kardec, who authored *The Spirits' Book*, was born in the city of Lyon, France on October 3, 1804. He was the son of Judge Jean-Baptiste Antoine Rivail and Jeanne Louise Duhamel.

From an early age, Hippolyte displayed a remarkable intelligence and keen sense of observation. He was fond of all subject matters related to Science and Philosophy.

He began his studies in Lyon and was sent by his parents at age 10 to study at the renowned Education Institute in Yverdun, Switzerland, directed by Pestalozzi, one of the great educators of that time.

It is said that as early as age 14, Kardec used to teach his younger schoolmates at Pestalozzi's Institute, where he was always an exceptional student. He later became an assistant, teaching the great educator's methods.

Around 1822, the young Rivail moved to Paris, where a distinguished career as professor was about to begin. While in Paris, he published several notable books, many of which were adopted by France's official educational system.

On February 6, 1832 he married Amélie-Gabrielle Boudet.

During the early 1850's Europe was swept by the widespread phenomenon known as "turning tables", which became a sensation throughout the aristocratic salons, especially in France. It consisted of a group of people gathered around tables, placing their hands on it with the intention to make them move. These experiments became a fad. The phenomenon was viewed as mere pastime, and there were no serious known attempts to explain what was really at work.

Towards the end of 1854, a hypnotist expert by the name of Mr. Fortier mentioned to Rivail that not only the tables "danced" and "turned" but they also answered questions!

Rivail, as a rigorous scientist, did not believe this activity. "I shall only believe it when I see it with my own eyes and when it is proven that a table has a thinking brain, nerve endings for sensations and can enter into a sonambulic state" he said.

In May of 1855, Rivail witnessed one of such "turning tables" meetings at the home of Mme. Plainemaison. There he observed that the tables would move, turn and reply intelligently, through knocks, to questions posed by those present.

Rivail decided to investigate the matter further. He took part in subsequent meetings at Mme Plainemaison's and continued researching and observing other gatherings at the home of the Baudin family in 1856.

During this time a great part of the preparation of *The Spirits' Book* occurred. Rivail was amazed by the answers given by the spirits to questions proposed by him through mediums.

On April 30, 1856, a medium called Ms. Japhet transmitted to him the first revelation regarding his mission, which would be to bring the Spiritist Doctrine to the world.

Rivail began the task with enthusiasm, and *The Spirits' Book* was written cataloging the transcription of questions asked by him of the spirits with responses received through mediums, along with comments written by him about the spirits' replies. Once the book was ready, the spirits recommended that Kardec reviewed the work thoroughly with the help of the medium Ms. Japhet, following the guidance of the Spiritual Plan, before sending it to the publishers.

On April 18, 1857, *The Spirits' Book* that represents a milestone not only in the records of Spiritism, but also in the history of our civilization, was finally released. To sign the work, Rivail chose the pseudonym Allan Kardec, a name that, according to his spiritual guide, he had during a previous incarnation as a Druid (an ancient people who inhabited a region of France and who believed in the immortality of the soul).

Preface from the Original Work

How this Book Came to Life*

In 1999 we began to study *The Spirit's Book* in our weekly home prayer meeting. We would gather our small family around a table on Sunday nights: my husband, our two sons and myself.

At that time, the boys were 10 and 12 years old and up to that moment had not been presented with any of the basic works of the codification. Our study groups had always been based on children's spiritist books, whether psychographed or not. However, the children were growing, and the children's books at our disposal started becoming less appropriate and unattractive to this pre-adolescence phase. They wanted more, and had the knowledge to go further. This was when we asked ourselves if it was time to introduce them to the study of *The Spirit's Book*. We knew the question was complex: after all, many of the subjects of this work of Kardec are adequate and understandable to youngsters of this age group, but some others might be difficult and outside of their realm of interest and /or comprehension. There was also another level of complication: Kardec was a 19th century scientist and philosopher and the language he utilized in his work reflected the times and his intellectual abilities, often being greatly above the vocabulary and level of comprehension of our pre-adolescents.

Even with such restrictions, we decided it was worth trying. And now, three years later, when we are almost finishing the study we began in 1999, we can assert that everything we had imagined was confirmed in practice. There are many portions of *The Spirit's Book* that awaken great interest in our boys (who are now 13 and 15 years old), but there are others whose themes still do not motivate them sufficiently or rather are so difficult for them to understand that they would become absent minded during the meeting. The complicated vocabulary caused a loss of interest. But, since I was the one reading aloud, I would always try to apply my practice as a writer to perform a 'simultaneous translation'.

That is, every time I read words or phrases that were out of their reach, I would substitute them for more colloquial synonyms instantly. This very experience led me to conclude that it would be opportune and useful to adapt *The Spirits' Book* for younger readers. And in this manner the idea for *The Spirit's Book for Young Adults and Beginners* was born. Based on the practical observations that I made during this time, I selected questions** that seemed most appropriate to the interests and universe of children and youngsters, 'translated' the language to bring it closer to standard codes and looked to fashion some unpretentious commentaries that could help to better understand the wise and profound teachings of the original work. Many of these commentaries are based on Kardec's observations themselves, and in shortened answers to questions not selected to be part of the book.

It is important to clarify that the selection of questions were based on personal criteria, always looking to perform good judgment and the experience acquired as an author of children's books as well as a mother of two youngsters, without attempting to exercise any type of censure or restriction. The adaptation of the text attempted to be honorable to everything that Kardec and the spirits had the intention of transmitting, always attempting to facilitate understanding and 'translate' the questions and answers to a simpler language. The introduction and conclusion of the original, as well as many of Kardec's commentaries, due to their complexity and length, were not hereby reproduced.

Finally, I would like to clarify that this work does not attempt in any manner to substitute the irreplaceable *The Spirit's Book*. It simply attempts to serve as a stimulus for young readers to later on, when they develop more maturity, fully engage into a complete lecture of the marvelous book written by Kardec.

The Spirit's Book for Young Adults and Beginners should be considered an introduction and an opening of a pathway, never an end in itself. If our young reader can begin to understand the truths and become fascinated with the most basic concepts within this book and if this leads him/her to desire to pursue further, I will have fulfilled my objective and task.

Laura Bergallo

First Causes

GOD

Kardec's question: What is God?
Spirits' answer: *God is the Supreme Intelligence, the First Cause of all things.*

With this, the spirits wanted to say that nothing would exist without God.

God is, therefore, the creator of all things, from the vast galaxies of the universe to the smallest grain of sand on the beach. He, who is the father of everything and everyone, created all beings, both those with life as plants and animals, as well as those of the mineral kingdom.

Kardec also explains that God is eternal, because he never had a beginning and will never have an end.

God is immutable because the changes that happen all the time in people's lives and in nature never happened to Him

God is immaterial because he is not made of matter.

God is unique because there are no other gods.

God is all-powerful because he can accomplish everything and because there is nothing and no one more powerful than He.

God is supremely just and good because his wisdom and kindness is revealed in the smallest things as well as in the largest.

THE GENERAL ELEMENTS OF THE UNIVERSE

Kardec's question: Can humans know the origin of things?
Spirits' answer: *No. God does not allow everything to be revealed to them here on Earth.*

Science has evolved tremendously throughout the centuries; and by doing so it is increasing humankind's knowledge. But the spirits have revealed that even the biggest advancements of science in this world are limited by the boundaries given to us by God. They also say that as we become better persons our knowledge and understanding of the mysteries that challenge our intelligence will also increase.

We know the cure to many diseases but there are many others still to be discovered.

We have been to the moon but there is an infinite universe full of stars yet to be explored.

Kardec's question: How may we define matter?
Spirits' answer: *Matter is the tie that binds spirits; it is the instrument that the spirit uses and upon which it simultaneously exerts its action.*

We know our body is made of matter. The spirit utilizes our body in order to live in the material world and be able to act over the material things that exist within it.

For instance we need our hands in order to plant a seed that will become a fruitful tree.

Kardec's question: What is spirit?
Spirits' answer: *The intelligent principle of the universe.*

In this way we can understand that we have a body; however we cannot say that we *have* a spirit within us. In reality, we *are* the spirit within as the spirit is the intelligent principle that "lives" within our body.

God, spirit and matter, together, form the "universal trinity", yet there is one more component that is neither spirit nor matter and is utilized by the spirit to exert power over the physical body. In order to ease our understanding we can compare this component to what we know as energy.

Kardec's question: Is universal space infinite or limited?
Spirits' answer: *Infinite. If it had boundaries, what would be beyond them? I know this baffles your reason, yet reason itself tells you that it can be no other way. The same is true of the idea of the infinity of the universe – you will never be able to comprehend it from your small sphere.*

This is a very complex matter because it is very difficult for us to imagine the *infinite.* And the spirits say that is just how it is;

there are things that we still cannot comprehend. For now it is enough that we understand that the universe's space is infinite. There is neither beginning nor end. Someday we will understand it better.

CREATION

Kardec's question: How did God create the universe?
Spirits' answer: *To borrow a well-known expression: by the divine will.*
Nothing can better exemplify that all-powerful will than those grand words from Genesis: 'God said, 'Let there be light, and there was light'.

The universe is God's masterpiece and according to the spirits it was formed by the condensation of matter that once was free in space; this happened by His will. After the disarray in the beginning each thing took its rightful place and the first living things appeared.
To make it easier to understand we can compare the appearance of these first beings to seeds that are dormant and eventually erupt to form a plant; or to a caterpillar inside its cocoon and when the time is right it comes out to become a beautiful butterfly.

Kardec's question: Did humankind first appear at various points on the globe?
Spirits' answer: *Yes, but at different periods, which is one of the causes of human race diversity. Later, humankind spread throughout the different climactic zones and new types arose in the course of alliances between different races.*

When speaking of the physical differences amongst the human races the spirits are clear that they exist only because of the different climates and customs.

As such variations of skin tones, for example, are due to the region where a people originated from, due to the climate and the intensity of the solar light exposure. This has even been proved by modern science.

Humankind is all equal and belongs to one single large family. They are all brothers in God and their path on Earth serves the same purpose.

Kardec's question: Are all the globes spinning through space inhabited?

Spirits' answer: *Yes, and contrary to what they believe, earthlings are far from being first in intelligence, goodness and perfection. Nevertheless, there are individuals who think they know the truth of the matter, imagining that this little planet is the only one privileged enough to be inhabited by reasoning beings. Pride and vanity! They fancy that God has created the universe only for earthlings.*

Our planet Earth is the fifth smallest of the eight plants that orbit around the Sun. In addition the Sun is considered a dwarf star when compared to the 400 billion stars that shine in the Milky Way. Our galaxy, the Milky Way, is one amongst the 100 billion other galaxies that science estimates exists in the universe. How can we be the sole inhabitants of such enormous space?

The spirits teach us that the different worlds do not have the same physical constitution and therefore can be inhabited by beings that are very different from us, formed by different types of matter and with other physical requirements. They use as an example the difference between fish, which were made to live underwater, and birds, which were made to live mid-air.

VITAL PRINCIPLE

Kardec's question: What happens to the matter and the vital principle of organic beings after death?
Spirits' answer: *The inert matter decomposes and is used to form beings; the vital principle returns to the universe.*

Kardec uses electrical equipment in order to explain the phenomena of life and death. The vital principle, or vital fluid, would be the electric impulse necessary to make the equipment functional. Without this electric impulse the equipment stops; without the vital principle our body dies. As we are aware our body decomposes after death (caused by the exhaustion of the organs in the body) and returns to nature.

The Spirits' World or the World of Spirits
SPIRITS

Kardec's Question: How may we define spirits?
Spirits' answer: *We can say that spirits are the intelligent beings of creation. They populate the universe beyond the material world.*

The spirits are the children of God and were created by Him. It is still a mystery to us when and how it took place. The spirits are beings who don't have corporeal bodies.

With our limited intelligence, we cannot understand very well what the spirits are made of. Kardec compares such difficulty of understanding to a person who was born blind and cannot imagine what light is like.

The spirits live in a world different from the one we perceive with our eyes — the spiritual world, which is a world that has existed even before our material world came into being. However, those two realms — the material one and the spiritual one — communicate and influence each other.

We have also been told that the spirits are everywhere and that they inhabit every corner of the infinite space. Many of them are around us most of the time and although we can't see them, they can observe and act upon us.

Kardec's Question: Do spirits have a specific, limited and constant form?
Spirits' answer: *To your eyes, no; to ours, yes. You might say that they resemble a flame, a glow or an ethereal spark.*

The brightness of that flame varies according to the level of purity of each spirit. Thus, the less pure are darker and more opaque, and the purer ones show themselves in a bright and vivid light.

Kardec's Question: Is matter an obstacle to spirits?

Spirits' answer: *No, they can pass through anything: the air, the earth, water, and even fire are all equally accessible to them.*

The spirits don't move around as laboriously as we do on Earth. They travel through space with the speed of thought, and nothing can block their passage.

They cannot be in two places at the same time, but depending on their purity, they can radiate their thoughts to many directions.

Kardec's Question: Is the spirit per se without a covering, or as some insist, is it surrounded by some kind of substance?
Spirits' answer: *a substance that might look vaporous to you but which is still quite dense to us surrounds the spirit. Nevertheless, it is sufficiently vaporous to be able to raise itself up into the atmosphere and travel to wherever it wants to go.*

This kind of "packaging" of the spirit is called perispirit, and it is different in the many inhabited worlds. When a superior spirit comes to our world, it needs to "dress" itself with a cruder type of perispirit; more adequate to the place it finds itself in.

The perispirit takes the form the spirit wishes and on many occasions we can see and touch it, while in dreams or even awake.

Kardec's Question: Are all spirits equal or is there some kind of hierarchy among them?
Spirits' answer: *They are of different orders according to their individual degree of self-purification.*

In the spiritual world the only characteristic that makes one spirit superior to another is its individual progress. There are spirits more or less advanced in every level. However, to help our understanding, we can classify the spirits into three categories. The first one is that in which the spirit has reached the top of perfection – the pure spirit, superior in intelligence and goodness. According to Kardec's teachings, that kind of spirit doesn't need to inhabit a material body, that is, it has no need to incarnate anymore. It doesn't have to undergo tests and atonements, and its happiness is complete. Its work is to help humanity and other spirits, and can be called angel, archangel, or seraphim.

The second category comprises the spirits that are still imperfect, but good. Because of their imperfections they still need to go through trials. They try to help humanity by showing the right path and protecting those who deserve it. They feel no hate, anger, envy, or jealousy, and can be called good spirits, guardian spirits, or spirits of benevolence.

The third category consists of those spirits who don't do good but neither do they cause evil, at least not as those who deliberately do evil to others. These are the ignorant, proud, and selfish spirits, although they are not all completely bad. Those spirits suffer a lot and know very little of the spiritual world. Some of them seek every opportunity to lead humanity astray and make them lag behind in their progress.

Of course, there are infinite variations within these three categories.

Kardec's Question: Are spirits good or evil by nature, or do they seek to improve themselves?
Spirits' answer: *They improve themselves, and as they do so they pass from a lower order to a higher one.*

The Spirits' Book teaches us that God created all spirits simple and ignorant, and gave them all a mission so that they can reach perfection little by little. On reaching perfection, each spirit will be close to God and will enjoy absolute happiness. All spirits, even the ones considered bad, will be perfect one day. That day will come faster for those who accept God's will and the trials they have to face without rebellion or desperation. No spirit, however, goes back on the progress already made; it may remain stationary for a while, but it never moves backwards.

Kardec's Question: Why have some spirits followed the path of goodness, but others the path of evil?

Spirits' answer: *"Don't they have free will? God does not create any bad spirits from the start; they are created simple and ignorant, that is, capable of both good and bad. Those who are bad have become so through their own will."*

Free will is the freedom that every spirit has to choose its own path. God leaves to each spirit the decision on what direction to take so that it can earn the fruits of everything it undertakes.

So, if one decides to be good, it will reap the rewards for its decision. The same happens to those who decide to do the contrary: their misconduct will turn against themselves. And, in both cases, the influence of other spirits will ensue – the imperfect ones will try to lead them towards negative actions; the good ones, towards the practice of goodness. The important thing is to know that each and every one of us is

THE INCARNATION OF SPIRITS

Kardec's Question: What is the purpose of the incarnation of spirits?

Spirits' answer: *God imposes incarnation for the purpose of leading spirits to perfection: for some, it is an atonement; for others, a mission. However, in order to reach this perfection, they must undergo all of the vicissitudes of corporeal existence – therein lies their atonement. Incarnation also has a further objective, which is to place spirits in conditions where they can do their share in the work of creation. On each world, they clothe themselves with an instrument that is in harmony with the essential matter of that world in order to execute in that instrument the orders of God. In this way, while contributing to the general work, they progress at the same time.*

We all play an important role in God's creation – a role that will help us in our individual evolution. In order to become pure spirits one day, we need to go through some ordeals, which purpose is to show us the path towards goodness. For that each spirit, in each incarnation, takes on a physical body adequate to the world it is going to inhabit. It is through that body and its interaction with the environment that spiritual progress is possible.

It is important to reemphasize that the spirit who chooses the path of goodness reaches the end of the journey faster and undergoes fewer sufferings.

Kardec's question: What is the soul?
Spirits' answer: *An incarnate spirit.*

It means that the soul is the spirit that occupies a body. And each spirit is connected to the body it occupies by a link that the spirits define as semi material, and which helps the soul to communicate with its body.

That link is the packaging we mentioned before, the perispirit. So, we may say that three parts form human beings: the material body, the incarnated spirit or soul, and the perispirit. As soon as a person dies, the spirit abandons the body because death breaks the links that connected them.

THE RETURN FROM THE CORPOREAL TO THE SPIRIT LIFE

Kardec's question: What is the soul transformed into at death?
Spirits' answer: *It becomes a spirit again; i.e., it returns to the world of spirits that it had left temporarily.*

When we die, the soul leaves our body and returns to the spirit world, where it had come from. The spirit keeps its individuality because it possesses a fluidic body that we call perispirit, which maintains the appearance the body had in its latest incarnation. It means that we somehow remain the same person we were when "alive", with the same flaws and good qualities, and even with the same image we used to see in the mirror.

Kardec's question: Is the separation of the soul from the body a painful process?
Spirits' answer: *No. Frequently, the body suffers more during life than at the moment of death; the soul itself feels nothing at death. The suffering that is sometimes experienced at the moment of death is pleasure for the spirit, for it sees that the end of its exile is at hand.*

This is the same as asking if dying hurts. And the spirits say that it doesn't. On the contrary, many times the disagreeable sensations that the spirit experiences at the moment of death are actually a reason for joy because they mean freedom from the body.

The spirits also teach us that the soul separates from the body little by little, and that the ties are undone, not broken.

Kardec mentions that the time the perispirit takes to untie itself varies from person to person, for more advanced spirits, it can be faster. For people who are too attached to material things, the spiritual disconnection may last days, weeks, or months, even though the body no longer has any vitality.

There are exceptional cases, as with suicide, in which the spirit may remain spiritually linked to the body for much longer, witnessing, with great suffering, the body decay that follows death. There are other cases where despite the soul having already abandoned the body, faint vital signs are still detected in the organism. These soon disappear, though. Besides the type of death, be it by accident or illness, the age of the being in which it occurs may influence the time the soul takes to leave the body.

Kardec's question: What sensation does the soul experience at the moment it realizes that it is in the spirit world?
Spirits' answer: *That depends. If it has done evil for the love of it, the spirit is at first ashamed of what it has done. However, it experiences something completely different if it*

has been morally upright. It feels relieved of a great weight and does not fear the most scrutinizing glance.

This answer gives us the certainty that the way we feel when we die will be pleasant if we have a clear conscience regarding our actions during life. In that case death means freedom, for we have nothing to be ashamed of and owe nothing to anyone that may be charged against us.

Kardec's question: Does a spirit immediately meet those whom it knew upon the earth, and who died before it?
Spirits' answer: *Yes, depending on the affection they had for one another. They almost always come to receive it as it strives to return to the spirit world and they may even help free it from the bonds of matter. It also sees many whom it had lost sight of during its stay on earth. Moreover, it sees those who are in the spiritual world and goes to visit those who are still incarnate.*

In cases of near-death experiences (NDE) studied by researchers, the meeting with relatives and friends already discarnate is often reported.

Near-death experiences (NDE) are those in which people enter in a state of clinical death but somehow recover from it and come back to life. They tell what they have seen and experienced when they were "dead". And many of them remember, with great emotion, having been received and supported by beloved beings at the door of the spirit world, exactly as the spirits describe it.

Kardec's question: Upon leaving the body behind, is the soul immediately conscious of itself?
Spirits' answer: *Immediately is not the right word; it remains in a state of confusion for some time.*

Such state of confusion, as mentioned by the spirits, depends on the stage of development of each individual. People too much concerned with the material aspects of life remain longer in this state; the more spiritualized ones, though, recover conscience more quickly. But almost all, as Kardec explains, feel as if they had been awakening from a long and deep sleep.

Also, in cases of violent death, this confusion may last longer, because people, at first, can't believe they are dead — after all, everything happened so fast that they didn't have time to get used to the idea. In addition, they don't "feel" dead because they think, hear, and see everything that happens around them.

For those who have known Spiritism, things may happen more easily; Spiritists, from their time of incarnate (or "living"), already learned how things come to pass. It can facilitate the process, but the spirits make a point in saying that the most important thing is to have practiced goodness and have a clear conscience, if one wants to have a good awakening after death.

THE PLURALITY OF EXISTENCES

Kardec's question: How can the soul that has not reached perfection during its corporeal life complete the work of its purification?
Spirits' answer: *By submitting to the trial of a new existence.*

The depuration – or purification – of the soul depends on the corporeal existences, or to put it simply, on the various lives that each one has to live. Thus, after having left the body — through the process we call death — the spirit needs to "occupy" again another body, in a new corporeal existence, in order to continue its purification. We call it reincarnation. And, the spirits tell us that the objective of the reincarnation is to make amends and the improvement of Humanity.

On each incarnation (or life) that we have, we move more or less forward (never backwards), towards our goal, which is to become pure spirits. It will eventually take place with each one of us, after the many incarnations we have to live, as many as necessary. We must never forget that the length of this path depends on us, and that at the end of that journey we will need to reincarnate no longer, for we will be the blessed spirits that Kardec has told us about.

Reincarnation is one of the greatest proofs of God's justice, for He always leaves us all an open door for repentance, no matter how bad we are still. So, if in one existence we have committed many mistakes, we will have the chance to redress all of them in the following lives, through the trials we will have to endure.

God wouldn't be just or good if he condemned forever people whom, most of the times, were born in unfavorable conditions and had a lot of difficulties to achieve the progress desired. We may use as an example the case of those who are abandoned by their parents as children and live under circumstances of total material and moral deprivation, with no one to give them education or teach them about the good path, and, consequently end up committing acts against the teachings of God in the adult life. As with us all – imperfect beings as well – they will also have new opportunities. And the experience lived will be entirely incorporated in their future lives.

Kardec's question: Are all of our different corporeal existences lived on Earth?
Spirits' answer: *No, not all of them, but rather on different worlds. Those on this globe are neither the first nor the last, but are the most material and the farthest from perfection.*

From this answer we understand that Earth is only one of the worlds we have inhabited throughout our various incarnations, and it does not stand amongst the most advanced ones. We also learn that, depending on our progress, we can live many lives in a same world, or live some incarnations in one world and then spend others in different planets, and that we can change worlds as long as we improve ourselves. In every planet that we incarnate, though, we always have the opportunity to move forward in our evolution.

Kardec's question: Do the beings that inhabit different worlds have bodies similar to ours?
Spirits' answer: *They undoubtedly have bodies, because the spirit must be clothed with matter in order to act upon*

matter. This envelope, however, is more material or less so, according to the degree of purity the spirit has reached. This is what determines the differences among the worlds through which we must pass, for there are many dwellings in God's house, and therefore many degrees. Some recognize this and are conscious of it here on earth, but others know nothing at all about it.

Kardec explains that the body is denser in less advanced worlds. In those worlds, physical needs are primitive. For example, on earth it is still necessary for us to destroy other beings (plants and animals) in order to feed ourselves.

In more advanced worlds, the inhabitants have less material bodies and more acute senses, and they experience higher moral development. No one there accepts the idea of harming another person; no one is selfish; no one has bad thoughts. Thus, they suffer much less because they make no wars nor do they fear death.

As we keep evolving, one day Earth will also be a place like those worlds. It is all up to us.

Kardec's question: Is the spirit of a child who dies very young as advanced as that of an adult?
Spirits' answer: *Sometimes much more so, because it may have had more existences and have therefore acquired more experiences, especially if it has progressed.*

It means that when a child dies, or discarnates at a tender age, it may be a spirit more advanced than its own parents. Even though it had no time to do either good or bad, its life might have been to "complete" a former existence that might have ended before the ideal time, and its death might also have served as a trial or atonement for the progress of the parents.

Actually, the death of young children, a relatively common fact, is another great proof of reincarnation, for where would God's justice be if He allowed some to die so young, and then go straight to Heaven, while others have to live longer and with more chances to make mistakes that could prevent them from entering that same Heaven? As Kardec points out, future happiness must be earned and reincarnation gives the same chances to everyone.

Kardec's question: Can a spirit who has animated the body of a man animate the body of a woman in a new existence, and vice versa?
Spirits' answer: *Yes, since the same spirit can animate both male and female bodies.*

Kardec says that spirits have no gender, and therefore they can incarnate as either a man or a woman. In that way, if in this life we have incarnated in the body of a woman, it is for us to experience situations that women go through and feel as they feel. In a future incarnation, as we animate the body of a man, we will live and feel situations typically as a man. Thus, we may advance more and learn to respect both genders.

Kardec's question: Since we have had many existences, does kinship go back to previous ones?
Spirits' answer: *It could not be otherwise. The succession of corporeal lives establishes ties among spirits dating back to former lives. Such frequently gives rise to the affinity between you and some spirits who you might think are strangers.*

Our relatives vary from one incarnation to another. Consequently, we have had different fathers and mothers in our past lives. Today we might have as a child someone who has been our brother, our uncle, our father, or our grandfather. It is possible that we have a great affection for someone in this life who is not blood related but who might have been our mother, for instance, in one or more past existences.

Blood ties, in general, are built on spiritual bonds that have been developed throughout the different incarnations. It is here that reincarnation, instead of weakening family bonds, strengthens them. This is because we know that we have been together for many centuries and that we will probably be together for many more. We begin to see people around us, even those who are not blood related at the moment, as possible relatives, from past or future lives.

We also learn, regarding genetic inheritance, that the body comes from the body, but the spirit doesn't come from the spirit. This means that we inherit physical traits from our parents, such as the color of our hair and eyes, or the shape of our nose, but our moral characteristics we inherit from ourselves, from one existence to the next.

However it is clear that parents can and should influence their children in everything that concerns their moral development as they are brought up. In fact, the spirits stress that this is the main mission of parenthood. It is why good parents can have problematic children. Their task is to help them become better.

Kardec's question: What is the origin of the extraordinary abilities of those individuals who, without any previous learning, seem to have an intuition about certain knowledge such as languages, mathematics, etc.?
Spirits' answer: *A memory of the past and the soul's previous progress, of which it now has no awareness. Where else could such abilities come from? Bodies change but the spirit does not. It merely changes its garment.*

We have all heard, or even known, someone who, since a tender age, has a knack for languages, or painting, or even for solving complicated mathematical problems, without having had any, or maybe just a little, formal training. Many of them are called wonder children or prodigies. In fact, they are only spirits who in their previous lives developed an ability in a special way and simply remember it, although they are not aware of the memory. After all, the spirit is always the same. It only changes "clothes" from life to life.

SPIRIT LIFE

Kardec's question: What becomes of the soul during the intervals between incarnations?

Spirits' answer: *It becomes an errant spirit aspiring to and awaiting a new destiny.*

The spirits say that the soul, in general, reincarnates some time (which can be short or long) after its previous life. In the superior worlds, however, reincarnation occurs almost immediately.

While it is not incarnated, the spirit waits for a new life. The wait may vary from a few hours to thousands of centuries, but one day the wait ends, and then the spirit incarnates again. Therefore, an errant spirit is one who, having finished one existence is awaiting the next.

There are errant spirits in every level of evolution but we cannot call the pure spirits errant because they no longer need to incarnate. Errant spirits study and try to progress acquiring new ideas that they will be put to the test in future incarnations.

Kardec's question: Are the perceptions and understanding of spirits unlimited? In other words, do they know everything?
Spirits' answer: *The nearer they approach perfection, the more they know. If they are highly evolved spirits, they know much. Little-evolved spirits are more or less ignorant about all subjects.*

This means that only the most advanced spirits have some real notion of the principles that govern the universe. And all of them, Kardec explains, live outside time as we know it, that is, the duration and the telling of time for them is very different from our own. What we see as a long time, a century, for instance, is very little time for spirits. According to their elevation, they have a sight that extends far beyond ours, enabling them to foresee the future, although they don't know everything.

Also, they don't need light in order to see. They don't need physical organs. They can see everywhere at the same time and hear sounds we cannot perceive depending on their state of purity. They are sensitive to beauty and good music, celestial music that is infinitely more beautiful than our own. They don't experience pangs of pain, cold, heat, or tiredness. Of course, we are talking about more advanced spirits. The lesser-advanced ones may still sense discomforts and suffer because, although they don't have the physical body anymore, the sensations seem too real for them.

Kardec's question: While in the errant state and before a new corporeal existence, does a spirit have the awareness and foresight of what will happen to it during its new lifetime?
Spirits' answer: *The spirit itself chooses the kinds of trials it will undergo. Its free will consists of doing so.*

From this answer we may conclude that God doesn't punish anyone. We ourselves choose our trials and therefore are accountable for their consequences. If we fail in any of the trials we have chosen God always gives us the opportunity to start the trials all over again.

The choices are made according to the type of wrongdoings we wish to redress with the objective of advancing quickly. Unlike what happens when incarnated, in Erraticity, errant spirits are able to understand the advantage of trials. Errant spirits see more clearly how much they can profit by going through trials that bring the progress they earnestly seek. It is like studying for a College Entrance Examination, choosing not to be distracted by invitations for movies and fun trips, in order to reach the higher goal of getting into the college and major of our choice.

Once inside a material body we often complain about our ordeals and wish not to have to go through them; we usually dream of a life that is only fun and games.

Kardec says that, in this sense, the material life is a copy of the spiritual one. Even when we find ourselves incarnated we must choose to let many things go so that we can achieve others we deem more important. And the spirit's sight, much keener than that of incarnates, is explained by Kardec as: a traveler at the foot of a mountain cannot see how much he has traveled and how far he still has to walk, but when he reaches the top of the mountain, he is able to see the whole length of the path taken and how much further he still needs to go. The traveler at the foot of the mountain is the incarnate with limited sight; the traveler on the top of the mountain is the spirit in Erraticity, capable of seeing much more.

Kardec's question: Can a spirit be mistaken as to the effectiveness of a trial it chooses?
Spirits' answer: *It may choose one that exceeds its strength, and then it succumbs. It may also choose one that will not be profitable at all; for example, a kind of idle and useless life. In such a case, however, upon returning to the spirit world it realizes that it has gained nothing and asks to make up for lost time.*

Again we are reminded that God never denies us another chance. If a chosen trial is too difficult, and we end up failing it, we will have another opportunity. The same is true when we don't use a given incarnation as well as we should and don't progress as much as we could have.

Choosing a profession, so important in the lives of young adults, along with the idea of a vocation, many times has everything to do with the decisions we make in Erraticity and with the progress we have already made in previous lives. Everything is linked. As incarnate or in Erraticity we are the same spirit following a unique and personal path chosen by ourselves.

Kardec's question: Do the power and influence that individuals enjoy on Earth warrant them any supremacy in the spirit world?
Spirits' answer: *No, because the lowly will be exalted and the great will be abased. Read the Psalms.*

The positions that people on Earth occupy, as well as their social and financial situations, are not repeated in the Erraticity. Among spirits, the authority that some exert over others is related to moral superiority and to the progress that they have already made. So, superior spirits, those who have advanced more, have authority over those who have progressed less.

The different orders of spirits have to do with their level of merit. Incarnates who have been powerful on Earth, such as influential politicians or wealthy individuals, may well belong to, and often do, the lower categories of spirits. At the same time, the most humble and poorest of their employees may be spirits of great elevation.

Kardec's question: Do all spirits have mutual access to one another?
Spirits' answer: *The good ones go everywhere and it must be this way in order to bring their influence to bear upon the evil ones. Nevertheless, the regions inhabited by the good ones are forbidden to the imperfect ones so that the latter cannot bring their evil passions there.*

Once good spirits have as their mission to help all the others they can move to the places where their help is needed. The malevolent spirits, who many times want to hinder the development of more inexperienced spirits, are limited to certain regions.

The communication among spirits is not made through words. It is established through the universal fluid that is the medium where their thoughts are transmitted.

The spirits recognize one another through the perispirit just as we incarnate know one another by means of our faces and material bodies. In this way we may be able to recognize those who lived near us when we discarnate.

Kardec's question: Do our relatives and friends sometimes come to meet us when we leave the Earth?
Spirits' answer: *Yes, they come to meet the soul they love. If it has escaped the dangers of the road, they congratulate it as though it has returned from a journey, and they help it to break free from its corporeal bonds. It is grace granted to the good spirits when those who love them come to meet them, while those who are soiled remain in isolation or*

surrounded only by spirits like themselves – it is a punishment.

The way we arrive at the spiritual world after death depends totally on the life we have lived. Thus, spirits that are mainly good, will be happily received by relatives and friends who have been waiting for them for a long time. On the contrary those who have chosen a path full of errors may be isolated having as their only company spirits who are equally bad.

It is important to point out that our choices in life will define our state after "death". It is in our own hands to make the right choices.

Kardec's question: Besides a general sympathy that results from various similarities, are there special affections among spirits?
Spirits' answer: *Yes, just as among humans; however, the link that unites spirits is stronger in the absence of the body, because they are no longer exposed to the vicissitudes of the passions.*

Kindred spirits, those who share a similar level of evolution, are attracted to and esteem one another. The esteem that exists among discarnates is even bigger than among incarnates because they are free from the demands of the body. Incarnates have needs and desires that many times hinder human relations.

However errant spirits can hate. This may happen with impure spirits who despise each other and incarnates too. They do everything within their power to foster misunderstandings and make people unhappy.

Hatred is not the rule, though. Even with people who have been enemies during their incarnations, "death" can bring the realization that the reasons that led them to enmity didn't have the importance they thought it had and the former enemies choose to reconcile.

In some cases, the memory of someone's evil doings against them may force the victim to stay away from the offender. Also, those who were abused by us while incarnate might forgive us if they are good and see that our regret is genuine. However, victims might maintain resentment and end up persecuting us for a long time even into subsequent incarnations. It is important to note that such persecution is only allowed if we deserve it.

Kardec's question: In what sense should we understand the term "other half", which certain spirits use to designate sympathetic spirits?
Spirits' answer: *The expression is not correct. If one spirit were another spirit's other half, it would be incomplete when separate from the other.*

The more perfect the spirits are, the more united they become, the bigger is their happiness.

Kardec teaches us that the so-called theory of the "other-half", which states that every one of us needs another half in order to be complete, is not correct. This is so because we are already whole. We don't need extra pieces to complete ourselves. What we need to do is to evolve towards perfection.

Of course, some spirits in the process of evolution are more akin to some than to others. A spirit leaving the inferior regions does not sympathize with those who have not evolved as it has because it no longer identifies with the ways of the spirits left behind. The sympathy that exists among spirits has to do with the likeness of their feelings, thoughts and inclinations towards good or bad.

The important thing is that upon reaching perfection all spirits be sympathetic to one another.

Kardec's question: Do spirits remember their corporeal lives?
Spirits' answer: *Yes, having lived many times as a human being, they remember what they have been, and I assure you that they sometimes laugh in self-pity.*

When we are free from the prison of the corporeal body we often reach an understanding of things far wider than we had on Earth. Consequently, we often laugh at ourselves as we remember petty things we gave so much importance to, the senseless acts we practiced and our immature behavior when incarnate.

After death we start remembering, little by little, not only our immediate former existence but also the ones before it. We especially recall those things that were really important and had some usefulness in our process of learning. It is then that we understand more clearly the true objectives of life and realize that our purification is the path that takes us to the infinite.

Kardec's question: How does a spirit regard the body it has just left behind?
Spirits' answer: *As an ill-fitting garment that has inconvenienced it, and which it feels happy to rid of.*

After an exhausting day of study or work we get home feeling hot and sweaty. It is such a pleasure to take those sticky wet clothes off because, at that moment, they have no more use for us. It is with a similar feeling that the spirits leave the body at the time of death. It is a relief to get rid of that body that had bound and hindered them and which has no more useful purpose.

Kardec's question: Do spirits hold onto the memory of the sufferings they bore during their last corporeal existence?
Spirits' answer: *They frequently do and this memory enables them to better appreciate the happiness that they now enjoy as spirits.*

When we die, we still keep remembering the good and bad moments we have been through in life. When we reflect on our sufferings we rejoice at having been freed of them. We also rejoice to find ourselves at another level of existence with a more complete type of happiness within our reach. Compared to such happiness, physical pleasures seem insignificant.

When in Erraticity, many of our notions and ideas are modified entirely. We begin to see clearly and to understand things from another far wider and truer point of view. The more dematerialized, or purified the spirit, the greater the changes in point of view.

Kardec's question: Are spirits sensitive to the remembrance of those who loved them on Earth?
Spirits' answer: *Much more than you may suppose. Such remembrance adds to their happiness if they are already happy, and consoles them if they are despondent.*

We may and should remember the loved ones that have departed ahead of us. Such memory is a proof of love, and brings great joy.

We may remember loved ones on special days, such as on All Soul's Day, but the date itself is unimportant. Likewise it doesn't matter if we visit their gravesite or if we pray for them from anywhere else. What make them happy are our thoughts.

THE RETURN TO CORPOREAL LIFE

Kardec's question: Do all spirits concern themselves with their approaching reincarnation?
Spirits' answer: *There are those who never give it a thought, who do not even comprehend it. It depends on the degree of their advancement. For some, uncertainty about their future life is a punishment.*

The spirits teach us that reincarnation is a necessity of spiritual life. Thus as long as we haven't reached perfection we will have to reincarnate.

Just as we are certain that we will die someday when we are alive, the spirits in Erraticity know they will have to reincarnate. Many don't worry about it. After all, how many of us worry about death even knowing that it will eventually come?

Kardec's question: Does a spirit have the right to choose the body it will enter, or does it only choose the kind of life that will serve as its trial?
Spirits' answer: *It may also choose its body, because the body's imperfections will be the trials that will help its advancement if it overcomes the obstacles it encounters thereby. This choice is not always up to the spirit, but it may at least ask for it.*

There are cases in which the spirit voluntarily chooses an imperfect body in which to reincarnate. The chosen imperfections may serve its evolution so it can evolve faster and achieve the lesson it set out to learn. However the decision on what body we will have lies in the hands of God. He may or may not grant our wish. Oftentimes what happens is the opposite. A still little evolved spirit may be imposed a body that will make its incarnation filled with the trials and atonements that it needs to progress, even if it hasn't wished it. Divine wisdom, ultimately, is what decides what is best for us.

Kardec's question: Is the moment of incarnation accompanied by a state of confusion similar to the one following discarnation?
Spirits' answer: *The confusion is much greater and especially much longer. At death, a spirit escapes slavery; at birth, it enters it.*

This shows us that many times things are the opposite of what our material mind thinks. In fact, being born is like going to prison; dying is to be free.

Thus, the period of confusion that a spirit goes through before incarnation is much longer than the one that occurs when it leaves the physical body through "death".

Kardec explains that the death of the body is for the spirit a kind of rebirth, and that reincarnation is a type of death.

Kardec's question: At what moment does the soul actually join the body?

Spirits' answer: The union begins at conception, but is only complete at the moment of birth. From the moment of conception, the spirit designated to inhabit a given body is connected to it by a fluidic tie, which gets tighter and tighter up to the instant the child is born. The newborn's cries announce that it has entered the number of the living and the servants of God.

Here we realize that life exists from the moment a man's spermatozoid fertilizes a woman's egg. The fluidic bond (a type of energetic link) that connects the spirit to matter is established right then and there. It is at that moment that the spirit who is reincarnating starts to bind itself to the new body. So we can understand that abortion, even when it is performed at the beginning of pregnancy, cuts short the trajectory of a spirit. Abortion prevents the spirit from reincarnating and facing the trials it was supposed to go through in the body that was prepared for it. Therefore abortion is a crime and an act of serious consequences that should never be practiced. The spirits only acknowledge abortion in cases where the mother's life is threatened by the continuation of the pregnancy or by the birth of the child.

The fluidic bond we have mentioned and which is established at fertilization grows stronger and stronger as pregnancy progresses. When the spermatozoid and the egg unite the spirit begins to feel confused and disoriented. Such confusion gradually increases until the moment of birth. During this period the spirit falls into a type of slumber during which its memories are erased little by little.

Kardec's question: Upon joining the body, does a spirit identify itself with matter?
Spirits' answer: *Matter is no more than the spirit's envelope, as clothing is the body's envelope. Upon joining the body, a spirit preserves the attributes of its spiritual nature.*

A good person is nothing more than a good spirit inhabiting a body. Imperfect spirits when incarnate become people who still do evil things or acts that show their ignorance of the laws of life.

The material body is like an outfit that the spirit has to wear and that serves as a tool for the spirit to act upon in the physical world. Its physical limitations are dependent on the state of the body's organs. For example, if the vocal chords of its body are damaged, the spirit won't be able to manifest itself in the physical world through speech, despite the fact that, as a spirit, it is not mute.

Regarding this, the spirits say we should not take an effect as a cause. They are saying that the material brain is not, contrary to what many think, what determines the intelligence and the moral qualities of a person. It is only the means for the intelligence to express itself in the physical world. Of course, if the brain suffers any kind of damage, such as a stroke, the person may be negatively affected and might not be able to communicate, speak, hear, or even reason. The spirit always remains whole but it just can't manifest itself through that body anymore.

A rough comparison could be when a TV set breaks down it no longer displays images or sounds even though the waveform signals in space may still exist perfectly.

Kardec's question: What is the usefulness of a spirit in passing through childhood?
Spirits' answer: *A spirit incarnates in order to perfect itself, and it is more accessible during childhood to the impressions it receives. This may assist in its progress. Those in charge of its education should contribute towards this goal.*

Being a child is very useful and needed for the incarnate spirit. It is during childhood that we learn more and are more open to the world's impressions and influences we receive. Hence the mission of parents or their substitutes is of great importance. These adults are the ones who can help to lessen our bad inclinations and to improve the good qualities we have already achieved. In childhood, the spirit is in a sort of repose, because

42

the physical organs are not yet fully developed. It is during adolescence that the spirit starts to repossess its own nature and shows what it really is. It is from this stage on that the spirit manifests its true way of being as a result of its many former incarnations.

The so-called child innocence is explained clearly in *The Spirits' Book*. It is only the temporary cover that hides the true being that inhabits the body that is growing up. The time of childhood innocence has great usefulness bringing forth the love and tenderness, especially from parents, that children need so much in order to be and feel cared for and protected.

Kardec's question: Why does the incarnate spirit lose the memory of its past?
Spirits' answer: *Human beings cannot and must not know everything. God, out of divine wisdom, wills it to be this way. Without the veil that hides certain things from them, they would be dazzled, like one who passes suddenly from the darkness into the light. By forgetting their past they are more fully themselves in the present.*

It is certain that, under normal circumstances, we have no memory of what happened to us, or of what we did in past lives. Such forgetfulness helps us in our evolution because it makes our adversities much easier to go through. It would be nearly impossible to pass our trials if we had the full memory of everything we had done. For example, imagine that a person had a fierce enemy in a former existence. Because of that reciprocal hate, they did much harm to each other. In the next incarnation, that very enemy is born as a child of the other. If both could remember everything that had passed between them, they would hardly reconcile and esteem each other as parent and child. Thus they would miss the opportunity to resolve the past problems.

However we always have a certain intuition regarding the events of our former lives. It is the conscience's clamor that attempts to prevent us from committing past errors and motivating us to do it right this time around.

In superior worlds, the forgetfulness of the past becomes less necessary. Elevated spirits have a clearer memory of their past existences.

Kardec points out that the spirit itself chooses the trials it will have to face in the new incarnation. If it prevails its prize will be spiritual progress. If it fails it will have to start over again. It is important to say, though, that a spirit never decays. It may go forward, or be stationary on its way towards elevation, but it does not regress.

THE EMANCIPATION OF THE SOUL

Kardec's question: During sleep does the soul repose like the body?
Spirits' answer: *No, a spirit never remains inactive. During sleep, the bonds that join it to the body are loosened, and since the body does not need it while sleeping, the spirit travels through space and enters into a more direct relationship with other spirits.*

The body rests during sleep, but the spirit itself is in full activity.

The spirits say that when we sleep we are momentarily in the same state that we will be after death. The spirit is free of the body, even if partially, and enters a state in which it can remember past lives and even foresee the future. It can also communicate with other spirits, incarnate or not, waking up with the impression that it had dreamed.

More elevated spirits, while sleeping, get together with superior spirits. They travel, talk, learn, and work. So, sleeping is like dying every day. If we are not afraid of sleeping why should we be afraid of dying?

The state of spirits during sleep, for example, where they go, what they feel and what they do, varies according to their individual progress just as happens after death. The lower ones might even visit regions inferior to Earth, where they can engage in less noble activities and consort with other spirits of the same level and with similar inclinations.

The dream is the memory of what the spirit experienced during our sleep, according to *The Spirits' Book*. But why don't we always dream? The truth is we do not always remember, or do not remember clearly, everything we see and do while asleep. This is so because we visit strange and unknown worlds during this period. Besides our physical organs aren't always prepared to keep certain impressions from the spirit. This explains in part why we sometimes have absurd dreams.

Bad spirits, which use our dreams to torment us, might provoke these dreams. This only happens, of course, because we somehow attracted them.

The detachment from the physical body that is caused by sleep may help spirits to communicate ideas that we usually think are ours when we wake up. These ideas might even make us sense the time, place, and circumstances of our own death.

The massive activity of the spirit could exhaust the body because they are linked together.

Kardec's question: Can two people who know each other visit each other during sleep?
Spirits' answer: *Yes, and many others, who think that they do not know one another, meet and converse. Without even suspecting it, you may even have friends in another country. The fact that during sleep you visit friends, relatives, acquaintances and individuals who may be useful to you is so frequent that you do it almost every night.*

Our social life during sleep is intense. We may meet people who are still incarnate and who are also sleeping to talk our problems over and help one another. Those meetings are quite useful, even though unremembered, because we will retain the intuition of a lot that passed and be able to use many of the ideas that came up on those occasions.

THE INTERVENTION OF SPIRITS IN THE CORPOREAL WORLD

Kardec's question: Can spirits know our most secret thoughts?
Spirits' answer: *They often know about what you would like to conceal even from yourselves, but neither acts nor thoughts can be concealed from them.*

The spirits can see everything we do and they can know our deepest thoughts. But they only pay attention to what interests them. When we think we are doing something hidden from everyone else, we must remember that there might be a multitude of spirits witnessing it.

Besides observing, spirits can also act upon our actions and thoughts. Their suggestions are often mixed with our own thoughts and most of the time it is very difficult to tell what thoughts are actually ours from what has been suggested to us. It is easy to know whether a suggestion, when it is the case, comes from a good spirit or an evil one. Good spirits only transmit good ideas and good advice. The bad suggestions can only come from evil spirits.

And why do evil spirits want us to do evil? Because they are jealous and can't stand seeing us well-balanced and happy. They want us to go astray from God just as they have done. God allows them to try to influence us so they can be instruments of our progress. They put our good decisions and our faith to the test. Still, we are never alone. On the contrary, the good spirits are always by our side to inspire us towards the good. We can clearly see that the final choice is ours. Our own mental outlook will determine if we attract good suggestions or bad ones.

Practicing good is therefore the best way to keep the evil spirits out of our lives and to attract the good and benevolent ones.

Kardec's question: Are there spirits who link themselves to particular individuals in order to protect them?

Spirits' answer: *Yes, spirit friends; what you call good spirits or guardian spirits.*

Our guardian angel is a protector spirit of high order. Its mission is to help us in the practice of goodness, cheering us up along the way, consoling and protecting us. This is just like parents usually do with their children. The guardian angel is dedicated to us from the moment we are born throughout our lives. Many times it stays by us even after we discarnate and throughout our various incarnations.

Even when we prefer to choose the influence of bad spirits, which is what happens when we decide to do evil, our guardian angel does not abandon us entirely. At those times it steps aside but still continues to inspire us towards goodness.

It is consoling to know that whenever we need it we have a guardian angel, a godsend gift and friend by our side that supports us in difficult times and gives us strength to resist evil.

In *The Spirits' Book*, the spirits of Saint Louis and Saint Augustine advise us to cherish that intimate relationship with our so important guardian angel. We must always be ready to listen to it and never forget to ask for advice and protection in every moment of our lives. From our guardian angel, who is our guide, we can hide nothing. It knows us intimately. It rejoices when we make progress and is sad when we fail. However, it is important to stress that we have our free will, that is, the final decision is always ours. Our guardian angel can inspire, advise, and encourage us, but the choice of what path to follow is made exclusively by us.

Kardec's question: Is a presentiment always a warning from a protector spirit?
Spirits' answer: *A presentiment is the inner and secret counsel of a spirit who wishes you well. It is also an intuition about a previous choice. It is the voice of instinct. Before incarnating, a spirit has knowledge of the principal phases of its coming existence; that is, the kind of trials in which it will be engaged. When these are of a marked character, it*

preserves a type of impression in its inner consciousness, and this impression, the voice of instinct, awakens when the moment arrives and becomes a presentiment.

Almost everybody has had some kind of presentiment or impression that is more or less vague that something is about to happen. The spirits teach us that such a presentiment might be advice from a friendly spirit or a warning that prepares us for something serious that is coming our way. The spirits also say that such a presentiment might come from us. This can happen because we become aware of the trials we are going to face before incarnating. This knowledge can leave such a strong impression on us that it remains even when we are in the physical body and this memory of the spirit comes to us in the form of a presentiment.

Kardec's question: Do spirits exert any influence on the events of life?
Spirits' answer: *Certainly, because they counsel you.*

We know that we are always being advised by our guardian angel and by other good spirits. These guiding spirits can also give us a hand so that certain things come to pass, especially what they consider to be good for us. That "hand" doesn't need to be nor is it always fantastic or supernatural. As Kardec illustrates, guiding spirits can make two people meet, though they think they met by chance, or make us pay attention to something that could have gone unnoticed but which will be of some importance to us later. Nevertheless, we cannot be reminded too many times that free will is above everything. The final choices are always our own. Besides, the spirits only influence matter in order to fulfill the laws of Nature. They never go against them. As we see in *The Spirits' Book*, whatever God desires to happen always comes to pass.

Kardec's question: Can't frivolous and mocking spirits provoke the little difficulties that defeat our projects and upset our calculations? In other words, aren't they the authors of what we commonly call the petty troubles of human life?

Spirits' answer: *They take pleasure in such annoyances, which are trials for you and are meant to try your patience, but they stop when they see that nothing comes of it. However, it would neither be just nor correct to blame them for all your frustrations of which you yourselves are the main authors by your own carelessness. Thus, if your dish breaks, it was probably due more to your clumsiness than the fault of spirits.*

Those inferior spirits, called by Kardec as frivolous and mocking, love to bother us and can be a real nuisance in our lives. However, such bothering is only going to take place if we, due to our own shortcomings, really have to go through it to serve as a trial to measure our patience and will only affect us in case we deserve it.

If that is not the case and we don't deserve it, the mocking spirits will eventually get tired and leave us alone because they don't see the desired results of their pranks.

Besides, we have to know what is provoked by that kind of spirits from what is our own doing. As we have seen in the previous answer, most of our problems are our own exclusive fault.

As for the incarnate that do us harm on Earth, many of them remain our enemies even after they die. In order to lessen such enmity, we must pray for them and always overcome evil with good. If they have no reason to hate us, one day they will understand that they are being unfair, and if they notice that they can't harm us, they will eventually give up. However, if they do have a reason to behave like that, sooner or later we will have to redress any wrongs we may have done to them.

Kardec's question: Can evil individuals, with the aid of bad spirits to whom they are devoted, cause harm to their neighbor?
Spirits' answer: *No, God would not permit it.*

Anyone who wishes to do harm against another can call upon inferior spirits to help them. However, the one who is to be harmed is able to get rid of any aggressions by the power of their own will because nothing they don't deserve will ever hit them.

Also, we must not forget that the inferior spirits summoned by someone to practice evil will ask a high price for that kind of help.

OCCUPATIONS AND MISSIONS OF SPIRITS

Kardec's question: Do spirits have any other duty besides their own personal improvement?
Spirits' answer: *They concur in the harmony of the universe and act as ministers in fulfilling God's will. Spirit life is a continuous occupation, but it is nothing arduous like that of Earth, because it is not subject to bodily fatigue or the anguish of need.*

All spirits, being inferior or superior, have something to do, a role to fulfill. They are all kept busy. Superior spirits though, instead of what happens with life and occupations on Earth, don't get tired nor do they get stressed.

All spirits have to inhabit various worlds and places and gain knowledge of all things, but all in due time. All spirits have to climb the ladder of elevation step by step in order to perfect themselves. The path to perfection is paved with knowledge acquired through individual effort and accumulated experience.

Even the more elevated spirits don't stay idle. They have the job of being God's emissaries carrying His orders throughout the universe. They are happy to do so because they love to be useful.

The missions and occupations of spirits of various levels are always according to the progress they have made. Each one is given a task it can perform.

Good spirits help in the progress of all humanity. They may take care of the sick and the ones close to death, help those in distress, advise all and inspire good thoughts. Of course, the good performance in these tasks helps them in their own progress.

THE THREE KINGDOMS

Kardec's question: What do you think of the division of nature into three kingdoms or into two classes: organic beings and inorganic beings? Some consider the human species as a fourth kingdom. Which of these divisions is preferable?

Spirits' answer: *They are all good. It depends on one's point of view: from a material point of view, there are only inorganic and organic beings. From the moral point of view, however, there are obviously four degrees.*

Kardec explains the four degrees that the spirits talk about. The first degree is the mineral kingdom of inert matter. The second degree consists of plants that have vitality. The third degree comprises the irrational animals, because along with vitality, they also have instinct. The fourth degree is the one to which human beings belong. The characteristics encompass vitality and instinct along with intelligence. Intelligence gives humans an awareness of their future, the perception of things beyond matter, and the knowledge of God.

Kardec's question: Do animals have free will?

Spirits' answer: *They are not simple machines, as you might suppose, but their freedom of action is limited to their needs and cannot be compared to human freedom. Since they are far less evolved than human beings, they do not have the same duties. Their freedom is restricted to the acts of their material life.*

The spirits say that animals have souls. Their souls are inferior to humans', but just as we do, they survive death and keep their individuality. Unlike humans, they are not aware of their own self.

Animals have no free will. With the death of the body, their spirits stay in Erraticity for a very short period of time. However, they cannot be considered errant because they don't think or act according to their will and have no conscience of the self.

Just as human beings, animals are subject to the law of progress. The spirits tell us that, in superior worlds, both human beings and animals are more advanced than on Earth. Human beings will always be superior to animals, as Kardec explains it, because of the intellectual and moral principles that the human beings have but animals don't.

Kardec's question: It has been stated that the human soul at its origin resembles the state of human infancy in the corporeal life, that its intelligence is only unfolding, and that it is preparing itself for life. Where does the soul accomplish this primary phase?
Spirits' answer: *In a series of existences that precede the period you call humanity.*

From this answer we can infer that the first stages of human spirit happen in the bodies of Creation's inferior beings, such as minerals, plants, and animals. And the spirits don't deny that possibility, explaining that everything is linked in Nature, and that the intelligent being that will eventually become a human spirit is prepared little by little during the time it animates those beings.

It is important to remember that, as it travels the path of progress, the spirit always passes from one inferior stage to a superior one. Its initial point, as Kardec puts it, is part of the origin of everything and is a secret that belongs to God alone.

Moral Laws

DIVINE OR NATURAL LAW

Kardec's question: What is meant by natural law?
Spirits' answer: Natural law is the law of God. It is the only true law necessary for the happiness of human beings. It shows them what they should or should not do, and they only suffer misfortune because they reject it.

The Law of God or Natural Law is eternal and unchangeable, as it exists from all eternity. Harmony, which exists in both the material and the moral universes, is based on Natural Law itself. The spirits teach us that all Natural Laws are Divine, since they are authored by God.

Kardec explains that among the Divine Laws there are Physical Laws studied by Science and Moral Laws, applicable to the actions that men and women practice among themselves, with each other, and to God.

For every new reincarnation, as we continuously progress, we improve our understanding of these laws. This is especially true with regard to the distinction between good and evil.

God entrusted certain individuals, superior spirits, with the important mission of disclosing His laws to humanity in order to promote progress of the world.

But in order to ascertain who those superior incarnate spirits are, the ones called prophets, we need to know how to recognize them. This is accomplished by observing their actions and words. They are always men and women of good will, inspired by God. The most perfect one among them, who is the guide and model for all humanity, is Jesus.

As for Jesus, Kardec says that he is the model of moral perfection that humanity can aspire to on Earth; he is the most pure spirit that has incarnated on this planet, the most perfect expression of God's laws.

Kardec's question: What definition may be given to morality?

Spirits' answer: *Morality is the rule of good conduct; in other words, being able to distinguish between good and evil. It is founded on the observance of God's law. Humans behave correctly when they do everything for the good of all, for then they obey God's law.*

Doing good is acting in accordance with God' law. Doing evil, on the other hand, is not following that law. To be able to distinguish between good and evil we use our intellect with reasoning. We have the means to make this distinction if we believe in God and follow His laws. So why does evil exist? The spirits answer is: because God allows people free will to make their own choices. We spirits need to experience both good and evil to learn from them. Therefore it is necessary to incarnate in a physical body to learn and grow. Superior spirits tell us that the evil is dependent on our will. This means that we are even guiltier when doing something bad if we know what we are doing. It is a matter of responsibility. To this point, Kardec says: an instructed and educated individual who commits wrongdoing is guiltier than the ignorant person who only follows one's own instincts.

It's not good enough not to practice bad deeds. The ideal is also not to desire it, but if we do, then we must resist to the temptation of practicing it. In addition, we must always look to practice the good, because when there is evil as a result from the good that we don't practice, then this will also make us guilty. As an example, if we choose not to help someone whom we could have helped, whatever bad happened to that someone who didn't get our help will make us guilty. The spirits remind us that not to do the good is already a bad thing.

THE LAW OF WORSHIP

Kardec's question: What does worship entail?

Spirits' answer: *It is the elevation of the thought towards*

54

God. Through worship, our souls draw nearer to our Creator.

We worship God as we recognize our weaknesses and need for His protection. There were never nations or groups that were atheists that did not believe in a Supreme Being. Worship has always existed in all groups and nations differing only in its form of expression.

The spirits teach us that true worship comes from the heart. In other words, when worshipping God there is no need for exterior and ritualistic manifestations, symbols, chants, ceremonies, or special places. The spirits, however, do not condemn these manifestations, as long as they express sincere feelings, and do not substitute for compassionate actions.

When Kardec asks if a ritualistic manifestation is a good thing, the spirits answer: *Yes, if it doesn't constitute in a simple fake action. It's always good to set a good example.* However we should always remember that God prefers sincere worshipper rather than the practice of mere ceremonies.

Worshipping God is about doing good and avoiding evil, following His laws and looking to think and behave according to His laws. This is particularly important for people who had a better understanding of divine truths. These beings are much guiltier for bad deeds they practice, the spirits advice.

Kardec's question: What is the general character of prayer?
Spirits' answer*: Prayer is an act of worship. Praying to God is thinking of God, drawing nearer to God, putting one's self in communication with God. Through prayer we may do three things: praise, ask and thank.*

To God, intention is most important. For this reason, the value of prayer is tied to its sincerity. Hence, God prefers prayer that comes out from our own self than a prayer that we only read, memorize, and repeat.

Those who pray with faith gain strength against evil and attract good spirits. It's not how much we pray that is important but rather the sincerity with which we pray, *The Spirits' Book* says. Through prayers we can be thankful to God and worship Him. We can thank Him for our lives and for everything that surrounds us. We can ask for something, which may or may not be given, provided we deserve and it provides us with a real benefit. Remember, what we believe is good for us, may or may not be true. Even when we don't get what we ask for in our prayers, we can receive strength and resignation, which will help us to face what cannot be changed.

As far as asking for forgiveness, a prayer is very useful. However, what really makes a difference is a change in our behavior showing an effort to try to correct our mistakes and wrongdoings. The spirits say that good actions translate into the best prayer because actions speak louder than words.

We can also pray for others. Sincere prayer can achieve the assistance from the good spirits for those we pray whether they are incarnates or discarnates. When we pray for the dead (discarnate), the prayer brings them a feeling of satisfaction and relieve. They understand that someone is concerned with their destiny and well-being. A prayer can bring them closer to regretting wrongdoings from their past, which will help to alleviate their suffering and attract good spirits and their counseling.

Finally, we can pray to the good spirits and to our guardian angel. As the messengers from God that they are, the prayers that we direct to them can only have effect if they are fully in accordance with the Divine Laws.

THE LAW OF LABOR

Kardec's question: Why is labor imposed on humankind?
Spirits' answer: *It is a consequence of their corporeal nature. It is an atonement and at the same time a means of perfecting their intelligence. Without labor, humans would remain in intellectual infancy. Thus, they must owe their food, safety and well-being to their own labor and activity.*

God has granted intelligence to those who are physically weak to compensate for it, but it is labor nonetheless.

Labor is a necessity that is part of Natural Law. It is through labor that we grow and acquire precious experience. The spirits teach us that labor is needed for the development of humans' thinking capability. That's why God wants us to depend on labor to be able to fulfill our material needs. Labor has two main objectives: preserve the body and develop intelligence.

Even the inhabitants of superior worlds work. Their labor may be one of less material exposure according to the world they live on. Contrary to what some may suppose, not to work in those worlds would not be an advantage; it would be an ordeal.

Rest is also part of Natural Law. We need rest to restore our bodily powers and free up our minds and intelligence a bit, in order for our thoughts to be raised above the physical matter.

When speaking of labor, Kardec brings up the topic of unemployment, which is always a contemporary one. To this point, the codifier says that the medicine for this issue cannot be found in economics theories. The medicine is in the moral transformation, which will give to *humanity behavior of order and providence for themselves and to each other, with respect to all that's highly regarded*, then avoiding *disorder and improvidence.*

THE LAW OF REPRODUCTION

Kardec's question: Is the reproduction of living beings a natural law?
Spirits' answer: *That is obvious; without reproduction the corporeal world would perish.*

Reproduction has an aim to provide new material bodies to Spirits who need to reincarnate.

Kardec's question: Are the human beings of today a new creation or the perfected descendants of primitive beings?
Spirits' answer: *They are the same spirits, who have returned to perfect themselves in new bodies, but who are still far from perfection. Thus, the present human race, which through its growth tends to invade the whole Earth and to replace the ones that are dying out, will also go through its period of decrease and extinction. Other more perfected races will replace it, which will have descended from the present ones, just as the civilized human beings of the present day have descended from the brute and primitive of early eras.*

We can see the Law of Progress in everything. We, contemporary and civilized human beings, were once the primitive and brutes who inhabited the Earth in the primitive periods. The current stage of humanity is much more advanced than the first humans, but as the good spirits say, it is far from perfection. We will be substituted by more advanced human races as we progress. This way we see that we are always moving forward.

Kardec's question: What should be thought about the means that are meant to deter reproduction with a view to satisfying sensuality?
Spirits' answer: *It proves the predominance of the body over the soul and how deeply humans are immersed in matter.*

This question approaches the contraceptive methods. The spirits, while not condemning them directly, say that their use demonstrates the materialist character that predominates among us.

Kardec's question: Is marriage – the permanent union of two beings – contrary to the law of nature?
Spirits' answer: *It is progress in the evolution of humankind.*

Kardec classifies marriage as *one of the first acts of progress in human societies.* Contrary to what happens to most animals (who don't have a partner for life), union through marriage brings humans fraternal solidarity.

The spirits do not see *absolute inseparability* of the marriage as a Natural Law. With this we understand that they acknowledge that separation may happen among married couples. However, they consider polygamy a social backwardness. Since the basis of marriage is affection that brings the couples together, and in polygamy there is only sensuality, this affection will not exist there. In addition, Kardec reminds us that, if polygamy were part of the Natural Laws, then there wouldn't be a certain balance in the number of people from each gender.

THE LAW OF PRESERVATION

Kardec's question: What was God's purpose in granting the instinct of self-preservation to all living beings?
Spirits' answer: *All beings must collaborate in the designs of Providence. That is why God has given them the need to stay alive. Besides, life is necessary for the perfection of beings; they sense this instinctively without perceiving it.*

The instinct of preservation, that involuntary impulse that all living beings have, is tightly coupled with the necessity of progress. As the incarnation is needed for our progress, we instinctively desire to stay in it.

God has given us the instinct to preserve life, working with nature to generate what is needed to maintain it. The careless actions of humans may adversely affect the availability of these means. This happens when we create unrealistic needs, take more than we really need, waste or abuse resources. In addition to humans' ambition, selfishness leads to unequal distribution with some people having so much and many others with so little.

Kardec's question: Is the use of the fruits of the Earth a

right of all humans?

Spirits' answer: *That right is a consequence of the need to stay alive. God would not impose a duty without granting the means to fulfill it.*

Using the fruits of the Earth is a right but it is also a duty, so that we can guarantee the continuation of life. However this use needs to come with a balance The spirits explain that God has put excessive enjoyment in front of us in order to test us and to teach us not to exceed certain limits. The limit of this excessive enjoyment must be tempered by necessity. When we go beyond this limit, for instance, eating excessively, we may be getting ourselves into illness conditions, or even death. This suffering is the consequence of free will, and not following the Law of God.

Kardec's question: How can people know the limit of what is necessary?

Spirits' answer: *Those who are sensible know it by intuition, but many recognize it at the cost of their own experience.*

When we eat too much, we don't feel well. Even when eating something that we really like we will regret going beyond the limit and start to feel sick. By intuition or by experience we have the capacity to avoid excesses, which are never good for our own body or soul. Those excesses could become vices and might affect others adversely, denying other's necessities. This goes against the moral sense and the sentiment of charity, which should guide our lives.

The spirits say that the desire for well-being is a natural thing. However we must never look for it at the expense of others in need.

THE LAW OF DESTRUCTION

Kardec's question: Is destruction a law of nature?

60

Spirits' answer: It is necessary for everything to be destroyed in order to be reborn and regenerated. What you call destruction is no more than transformation that is aimed at renewing and improving living beings.

On Earth we have a distorted and usually negative view of all destructive processes. Yet these processes are absolutely necessary for the continuation of life. Some beings can only survive with the destruction of others. Herbivores eat plants and carnivores eat other animals.

For living things to continue procreating it is necessary that those who came before move on. Without destruction there would be an uneven distribution of beings in the world that would prevent the continuation of life for all.

It is important to remember that the essential, the spirit, can never be destroyed. But in order for it to transform and evolve it is imperative that the material portion, the physical body that surrounds it, is destroyed through death.

Kardec's question: Since death should lead us to a better life and deliver us from the ills of this world, and is therefore to be desired instead of dreaded, why do humans have an instinctive horror of it, making it a cause for apprehension?

Spirits' answer: We have already stated that humans should seek to prolong their life in order to accomplish their task. That is why God has given them the self-preservation instinct, which sustains them in all their trials. Without it they would frequently give in to discouragement. The secret voice that tells them to repel death also tells them that they may yet do something more for their progress. When danger threatens them, it warns them that they must take advantage of the time that God has granted them. But ingrates usually give thanks to their lucky star instead of their Creator.

The conservation instinct keeps us moving forward through life's tribulations and is what leads us to try and avoid death. It allows us to continually fight for our constant progress. When

61

we avoid danger's way we are ecstatic knowing we can continue the mission given us before we incarnated. We cannot forget, however, that when we win the battle over a serious danger, it is God giving us an opportunity to continue evolving. Therefore, we must use these opportunities wisely.

Kardec's question: In their present state, do humans have an unlimited right of destruction in regard to animals?
Spirits' answer: *That right is limited to the need of providing for their food and safety. Abuse has never been a right.*

What the spirits mean to remind us is that we are entitled to the destruction of animals with the intent of survival and safety. It is our right to destroy animals that we use for our feeding, since eating meat is part of our current evolution level, or to defend ourselves from attack. But it is an abuse and a violation of God's laws to destroy life for any other reason. All unnecessary destruction provoked by us on Earth will be accounted for.

Kardec's question: For what purpose does God inflict humankind with destructive calamities?
Spirits' answer: *To impel them to progress more quickly. Haven't we stated that destruction is necessary for the moral regeneration of spirits, who acquire a new degree of purification during each new existence? You must see the end in order to appreciate the results. You only judge such things from your own personal point of view, and you regard such inflictions as calamities because of the injury they cause you. However, these hardships are often necessary in order to make things arrive at a better order more quickly, and to accomplish in a few years what would otherwise require many centuries.*

Even the great tragedies that impact large masses of people at once (such as an earthquake, a great fire, a flood, tsunami and epidemics) have great purpose to progress. The way we look at these things make them seem bad. In reality they speed up Humankind's evolution. Great tragedies, however, can exist because of people's own attitude and resistance to learn to do good. We cannot overlook the fact that a major part of these tragedies may be a consequence of the individual's own irresponsible attitudes, destroying forests, polluting water and air, disrespecting nature and one another.

Tragedies are trials for individuals who have the opportunity to be patient and accept things they cannot change as well as practice solidarity and kindness towards others as they assist those in need in painful moments.

Kardec's question: What is the cause that leads humankind to war?
Spirits' answer: *The predominance of the animal nature over the spiritual, and the satisfaction of their passions. In the state of barbarity, nations only know the right of the strongest, and that is why war is a normal state for them. As humans evolve, war will become less frequent since they will avoid its causes, and when it does become necessary, they will know how to make it more humane.*

The spirits give us good news: someday wars will disappear from the face of the Earth. This is going to happen whenever all peoples of the planet practice God's Justice and Laws. They will then become brothers and sisters.

Until this happens wars will continue to take place on the planet and bring with it pain and sorrow. Only the spiritual progress of humankind can prevent war from happening as humankind evolves and we learn to be less barbaric and more diplomatic in order to solve disagreements.

Kardec's question: Is murder a crime in God's sight?
Spirits' answer: *Yes, a great crime, because those who take the life of another fellow being thereby cut short a life of atonement or mission – hence the evil.*

When someone is murdered something very important is interrupted. The victim ceases his evolutionary existence and misses out on a unique opportunity to progress. The killer is responsible and committed not only for his victim but also towards divine law. The murderer's actions bring about serious consequences to both in their evolutionary progress.

Kardec's question: Will the death penalty someday disappear from human legislation?
Spirits' answer: *The death penalty will assuredly disappear and its suppression will signal progress for humankind. When humans become more enlightened, the death penalty will be completely abolished on the Earth. They will no longer need to be judged by others. I speak of a time which is still very distant for you.*

Kardec mentions that though we are still far from becoming the ideal society some things have been improving. In the countries where the death penalty is still legal, the decision is no longer simple or cruel as it was before. Prisoner torture in the name of justice had been considered a normal action amongst many peoples, yet today it is rejected as a barbaric attitude. This shows that Humankind as a whole is advancing and meliorating. The spirits remind us that we should give prisoners a second chance to repent and Jesus preached forgiveness, not vengeance. Besides, no one escapes the Divine Justice that always leads us to learn by experiencing the consequences of the errors we make, going through the same pain we bring others in this or future incarnations.

The existence of the death penalty is a direct result of the low advancement state in which we still find ourselves. We must fight for its abolition.

THE LAW OF SOCIETY

Kardec's question: Is societal life natural?
Spirits' answer: *Certainly. God has made humans for living in society; otherwise, God would not have needlessly given them speech and all the other faculties necessary for a life of relationships.*

As we live in society we learn to fight off selfishness and to aid others towards evolution. That is how Humankind advances. If we each lived in isolation we would have no resources to progress. It is through the experiences that we gain living together that we improve our character and contribute to the betterment of those around us.

Kardec's question: What would be the result for society if family ties were relaxed?
Spirits' answer: *A magnification of selfishness.*

Contrary to animals who take care of their cubs only until they can manage on their own to the point of not even recognizing each other later on, humankind keeps a much closer relationship with children. The spirits tell us this happens because animals act out their survival instinct while we act out our need to progress. Progress is only possible through social ties and family ties are the tightest of them all. Through family we learn to love one another.

THE LAW OF PROGRESS

Kardec's question: Do humans draw from within themselves the power to progress, or is progress nothing more than the result of education?
Spirits' answer: *They advance naturally by themselves. Not all progress at the same time or in the same manner, however, and it is through social contact that the most advanced help others to progress.*

If each individual takes his or her own time to advance and do it in a particular manner, we assume progress depends more on each individual than on Nature. Spirits advise that intellectual progress, intelligence and knowledge, leads to moral progress, good character and principles. When individuals advance in intelligence and knowledge they better comprehend good and evil and are better able to distinguish one from the other.

This means that there may be individuals and nations intellectually brilliant but morally immature. The responsibility of those intellectually developed is greater since they are able to understand the world around them. The actual purpose is complete progress, intellectual and moral. This can only be achieved throughout time along with incarnations.

Kardec's question: By what signs may one recognize a completed civilization?
Spirits' answer: *You will recognize it by its moral development. You believe yourselves to be very advanced because you have made great discoveries and wonderful inventions, and because you are better situated and better clothed than primitives. However, you will only have the right to truly call yourselves civilized when you have finally banished the vices from your society that dishonor it, and when you finally live as brothers and sisters by practicing Christian charity. Until then, you are really no more than enlightened cultures that have only passed through the first phase of civilization.*

Kardec explains that the degree of civilization of a nation depends on the moral progress reached by its people. Thus, the more civilized a society the less selfishness, greed and arrogance it will have.

In a truly civilized society all will practice Jesus' teachings, all the time. In this society, intellectual and moral matters will always be above material matters. Intelligence will be freer. Sentiments such as goodness, generosity, good faith, respect for others' life, beliefs, opinions and the weak will be protected. Justice will be fair and basic necessities will not lack good-willed persons.

Kardec's question: In what way can Spiritism contribute to progress?
Spirits' reply: *By destroying materialism – one of the sores of society – it enables people to comprehend where their*

true interests lie. Since the future life is no longer veiled by doubt, men and women will better understand that they can ensure their future through the present. Destroying the prejudices of sect, caste, and color, it teaches them the great solidarity that must unite them as brothers and sisters.

This transformation, which the spirits say will be a work of Spiritism, cannot happen all of a sudden. Change of concepts only happens little by little. Change in humankind usually takes generations to occur. But everything will be transformed in time. Spiritism is here to help with steps within our reach. We can progress by trying to amend our faults as we advance through the doctrine's knowledge.

THE LAW OF EQUALITY

Kardec's question: Are all people equal before God?
Spirits' answer: *Yes, all tend towards the same goal, and God has made the divine laws for everybody. You often say, 'The sun shines on everyone' and you thereby state a greater and more general truth than you might think.*

No person is naturally superior to another. Rich or poor everyone is born with the same aims and all go through their paths of suffering. All bodies are destroyed by death, as Kardec teaches, and all individuals are equal in the eyes of God.

With this conviction we observe that prejudices of race, social classes, beliefs and so many others are totally absurd and demonstrate the level of continuous moral delay in our society.

It is certain that some people are more skillful at some things than others. This difference is a result of each one's effort and free will in this current life and past lives. Our greater individual development, therefore, depends only on our own will, as personal "gifts" are the result of our efforts throughout incarnations.

Kardec's question: Is the inequality of social conditions a natural law?

Spirits' answer: No, it is the work of humankind, not of God.

The spirits remind us that inequality should disappear as people advance and humankind stops being arrogant and selfish. Social inequalities provide people with different situations in each incarnation. Thus an individual who is born wealthy in one life may come back very poor and vice-versa. Positions alternate so we can learn all the lessons we need to succeed spiritually. In conclusion, social inequalities should have an end on our planet when they are no longer useful to our evolution. That is, when arrogance and selfishness no longer exist on the face of the Earth.

Kardec's question: Which of these two trials is more dangerous to humans: poverty or wealth?

Spirits' answer: *They are equally so. Poverty provokes complaining against Providence, whereas wealth leads to all kinds of excesses.*

The spirits, as well as Kardec, assert that wealth is very difficult. Wealth as a trial has a double edged sword. After all, to whom much is given much is expected. How one deals with good fortune determines moral growth. If our goal is moral improvement, the opportunities and power offered by wealth may not always constitute the shortest path. Beings have much more means to do the good. However, humans can become greedy and selfish, inappropriately employing the resources God has given them and postponing their personal duties and growth. Wealth is intimately connected to materialism that can divert the individuals from their truly spiritual nature.

Kardec's question: Are men and women equal before God and do they have the same rights?

Spirits' answer: *Hasn't God given them both the knowledge of good and evil and the faculties for progress?*

By answering Kardec's question with another question the spirits have given us a very clear answer. They explain that the existing position of considering women inferior to men in certain societies is the result of moral delay and only happens for cultural reasons. Women frail physical constitution in relation to men's by no means represent a sign of inferiority but rather that they have different functions to perform during physical life. Men are physically stronger and can perform heavy tasks. Women have sensibility and delicacy necessary for motherhood and other important tasks.

The spirits clearly tell us that the emancipation of women follows civilization's progress and that both men and women must have the same rights. They also point out that in each existence we can incarnate in feminine or masculine bodies. This proves that gender alternation is a feature of the material world.

THE LAW OF FREEDOM

Kardec's question: What would be a condition in which humans could enjoy absolute freedom?
Spirits' answer: *That of a hermit in the desert. As soon as there are two individuals together, there are rights to respect, and they therefore no longer have absolute freedom.*

The spirits say that we all need one another, regardless of our status as children or adults, rich or poor, humble or powerful. This condition makes living with others necessary and to make it possible we must respect one another's rights. Respecting such rights means giving up, many times, our individual freedom.

A very simple example would be to maintain silence of a public library. A person might wish to read aloud. If absolutely free one would do as one wished. But it is necessary to respect other's rights to have a quiet area to concentrate on their own readings. Therefore, individual freedom is limited by other's rights and needs. For this reason there is no absolute freedom.

Kardec's question: Is every belief respectable, even when notoriously wrongheaded?
Spirits' answer: *Every belief is respectable when it is sincere and leads to the practice of goodness. Reproachable beliefs are those that lead to evil.*

We learn from the spirits the importance of conscience freedom, that is, freedom of thought and belief. Thus, we must always respect other people's thoughts and, consequently, their beliefs, which will be respectable if they lead to the practice of good.

Kardec's question: Do humans act with free will?
Spirits' answer: *Since they have freedom of thought, they have freedom of action. Without free will, human beings would be machines.*

Free will is the capability that every individual has of choosing his or her acts. The spirits remind us that the more developed an individual the more responsible they become for their choices. The conscience guides free will. Progress depends on choices made as well as the time taken for their progress.

Kardec's question: Is there fatalism in the events of life according to the meaning attached to that word; that is, are all events predetermined, and if so, what becomes of free will?
Spirits' answer: *Fatalism only exists when applied to the choice made by spirits upon incarnating to undergo this or that trial. Upon choosing a particular trial they delineate for themselves a kind of destiny, which is the proper consequence of the position in which they now find themselves. I am referring only to trials of a physical nature. As for moral trials and temptations, spirits preserve their free will to choose good or evil and are always able to yield or resist. When good spirits see individuals lose courage, they may rush to their aid but they cannot*

influence them to the point of eclipsing their will. An evil spirit, that is, a little evolved one, can disturb and frighten them by exacerbating a physical danger. Whatever the circumstances, however, the incarnated spirit still retains its entire freedom of choice.

What we may consider a calamity or misfortune may actually be life's events with which we must deal. Many times these are the result of our choices before incarnating and consequences of our own acts, for the sake of our evolution.

None of this is capable of surpassing free will. Thus, humans are capable of choosing their own path and such choice will determine what they will go through in their present life and future incarnations.

Sowing is free, harvesting is compulsory. This means that we can choose what to sow, but we can only harvest what we have sown. Whatever is the "fate" humans establish for themselves by their free will, the spirits assert that only the moment and the way of death are truly fatal. We cannot escape from that moment and nothing can prevent our death when it is time for us to leave. On the other hand, there is not any danger, as great as it may be, that would take us before the right time. It is interesting to observe that we often foresee how and when we are going to die – as, when we are spirits, before taking a new body, this information is often revealed.

Other events are the consequence of our past free will and may often be modified or avoided by our current free will. Thus, we should take the responsibility for our choices and their outcomes. We establish our own "fate". The power to live life better is, therefore, in our hands.

Kardec's question: Can the future be revealed to humans?
Spirits' answer: *In principle, the future is hidden from them and only in rare and exceptional cases does God permit it to be revealed.*

Being aware of the future would paralyze us. If we knew that a certain event would happen in a determined way, what vantage would we have to fight and change things? The awareness of the future would not be helpful to our evolution, as it would jeopardize our free will, making us passive and impotent.

THE LAW OF JUSTICE, LOVE AND CHARITY

Kardec's question: How may justice be defined?
Spirits' answer: *Justice consists in respecting the rights of others.*

The spirits teach us that a feeling for justice has always existed in humans' hearts, and it was God who put it there. Moral progress may help to develop it, but culture does not determine its intensity. There are humble, almost illiterate individuals, who have inside them a feeling for justice much more intense than others more literate.

The Spirits' Book defines justice as the respect for others' rights. But what determines these rights? The spirits tell us they are determined by both human and natural law. Human law is flexible as time goes by. As people develop the law also develops. It is also imperfect and does not always expresses justice with accuracy, only regulating social relations.

True justice is a matter of conscience and it may be understood in the following of Christ's saying, which is very simple to understand: *Do unto others as you would have others do unto you.*

Kardec's question: Does the right to stay alive give them the right to accumulate what is needed to live on and retire when they can no longer work?
Spirits' answer: *Yes, but they must do this as a family – like the bee – through honest labor, and not accumulate assets as selfish individuals. Certain animals set an example of such foresight.*

Considering that, as taught by the spirits, human's first natural right is the right to stay alive, should they accumulate assets in order to rest at old age? The answer is yes, under the condition that this asset accumulation is done by honest and not-selfish means. Spirits also say that ownership resultant from labor is a natural right, and it is as sacred as the right of working and living.

However, such ownership can only be considered legitimate before the divine law if it is achieved by not harming others, and one must always take into account the practice of love and charity. God does not take kindly the accumulation of useless assets, just for ambition – forgetting our fellow beings' necessities – even if it is in accordance with human laws.

Kardec's question: What is the true meaning of the word charity, as Jesus understood it?
Spirits' answer: *Benevolence towards everyone, indulgence towards the imperfections of others and forgiveness for offenses.*

Kardec explains that love and charity complement the law of justice. To love our fellow being means being benevolent towards them as much as possible, as we wish others to be benevolent towards us. He reminds us that charity is not only alms giving and it must be part of every relationship we have, whether with people in the same, above or below our social condition.

Charity is the attempt of never humiliating others, of always forgiving their imperfections and offenses and of trying to elevate people in inferior conditions to be closer to ours. As for the enemies, if we cannot love them yet, as Jesus used to say, we must at least try to forgive them, never take revenge on them, and always give good in return to what they have done.

MORAL PERFECTION

Kardec's question: Which is the most meritorious of all the virtues?

Spirits' answer: *All virtues have their merit, because all are signs of progress on the moral path. There is always virtue when there is voluntary resistance to the allure of evil tendencies. However, the highest virtue consists in the sacrifice of self-interest for the good of one's neighbor without ulterior motives. The greatest merit is that which is based on the most disinterested charity.*

Acquiring virtues is something we achieve throughout incarnations. When we overcome the disposition to practice evil, the good becomes a simple habit and good feelings triumph without the need of great effort from us.

We are, however, still very far from perfection and most of the times good is an exception. But Spirits tell us there are many worlds more advanced than ours, where charity is truly put into practice. In such worlds good is a rule, evil is the exception. In these worlds, good is spontaneous and happiness is predominant among the good spirits living there. Detachment from material matters and disinterestedness in good actions are pointed out in *The Spirits' Book* as important virtues that lead to evolution.

Kardec's question: **Since the corporeal life is only an brief stopover on this world and since our future life should be our principal concern, is it worthwhile to put forth the effort to acquire scientific knowledge that only bears upon material things and necessities?**

Spirits' answer: *Undoubtedly. First, it enables you to help your brothers and sisters. Next, your spirit will evolve more quickly if it has progressed intellectually. In the interval between incarnations you will learn in one hour what would require years on Earth. No knowledge is useless; it all contributes in some degree to advancement, because the perfect spirit must know everything. Since progress must be made in every sense, all acquired ideas help the development of the spirit.*

Study is essential to our spiritual progress. Acquiring knowledge of things of the material world also helps our evolution, because the development of our intellect contributes to moral perfection. Furthermore, scientific knowledge is important to peoples' progress.

Kardec's question: Could humans always overcome their evil tendencies through their own efforts?
Spirits' answer: *Yes, and sometimes with very little effort; what they lack is will power. How few of you make such an effort, however!*

This illustrates, again that it is our choice. It is possible to fight evil that still persists within us through our efforts. Nonetheless, we are not used to make efforts as much as we could. We shall remember: our evolution depends on our disposition to put forth efforts for good's benefit.

Kardec's question: Among all the vices, which may we regard as the root?
Spirits' answer: *We have already told you many times: selfishness. All evil derives from it. Study all the vices and you will see that selfishness is at the bottom of them all. As much as you struggle against them, you will never uproot them as long as you have not destroyed their cause. Let all your efforts tend towards that end, because selfishness is the true scourge of society. Those in this life who want to approach moral perfection must uproot from their heart every sentiment of selfishness, for selfishness is incompatible with justice, love, and charity; it neutralizes all other qualities.*

Selfishness lessens as we withdraw from materialism and seek to become more spiritual. Instead fighting against selfishness many human institutions end up encouraging it.

Our moral inferiority, so connected to the value we add to things, is the cause of selfishness. In the same way we gradually reject other moral imperfections, we may also become less selfish as we become less imperfect. There are very selfish people on Earth, but there are also people who are already overcoming this obstacle.

The day selfishness is banished from human environment, solidarity will prevail and all will live as brothers and sisters, helping each other and never practicing evil. As spirits tell us, when this day comes, the strong will assist the weak instead of oppressing them, and no one will lack the bare necessities of life, for society will be fairly structured.

Kardec says that selfishness can only be overcome through education. "It is through Education, even more than by Instruction that Humanity will be transformed. Not the education that turns people into instructed and lectured individuals, but the education that is the key of our progress, the education that conceives good individuals." Kardec also says that when humans understand that selfishness is the cause of all evil, and that it generates feelings such as envy, jealousy, arrogance and hate, they will also understand that happiness cannot exist while there is selfishness. Then, they will banish it from their lives by their own will power.

Kardec's question: What is the most effective means for improving ourselves in this life and for resisting the draw of evil?
Spirits' answer: *A sage of antiquity has told you: 'Know thyself'.*

But how can we achieve this? – Kardec asks. And the spirits advise him in a very simple way: at the end of each day, we must examine our conscience. We must remember what we did during the day, asking ourselves if we did not let any accomplishment aside or if anyone has reasons to complain about us. So, we can honestly find out our faults, identifying what we need to change.

The spirits tell us that we should ask ourselves: "if I die now, will I come back to the spiritual world, where nothing can be hidden, fearless to account for my actions"?

Self-knowledge is fundamental to the individual progress, but it is not easy to judge ourselves. How can we truly learn if our actions are good or bad, as we have the tendency of excusing everything we do? The solution is, again, quite simple: we just have to judge our actions as if others were practicing them. Listening to what others think of our actions (including the enemies) also helps.

All this is part of a daily work addressed to our evolution. Always asking our conscience about our daily behavior is the fastest and most efficient way to self-knowledge and, in consequence, to the achievement of the happiness we all desire.

Hopes and Consolation

EARTHLY JOYS AND SORROWS

Kardec's question: Can human beings enjoy complete happiness while on Earth?
Spirits' answer: *No, because life has been given to them as either a test or an atonement, but it depends on them themselves to mitigate their misfortunes and be as happy as possible while on Earth.*

Spirits speak plainly that even the relative happiness we can accomplish on Earth depends only on ourselves. Nearly always, we are the leading cause of our own unhappiness, which can be withdrawn by practicing the law of God. After all, our misfortunes are consequences of our deviation from the straight path.

So how can we define happiness? To spirits, material happiness is having the necessary, and moral happiness is having peace of mind and belief in the future. If we truly wish to be happy, we should look after those who materially have less than us. Fortunate are those who have simple aspirations and do not envy those who, apparently, are more favored than them. Spirits are very clear regarding this matter: the richer individual is not the one who has more properties, but the one who has fewer necessities.

With regard to moral happiness, we can only make it possible in the absence of feelings such as pride, envy, jealousy or greed– true afflictions that deprive individuals of peace. In fact, all our misfortunes are related to materialism. For if we are really capable of raising our thoughts to the infinite, all the material issues will seem insignificant and may not cause us any sort of suffering.

Kardec's question: Doesn't the loss of loved ones cause us suffering and a legitimate source of sorrow, since such loss is both irreparable and independent of our will?

Spirits' answer: *This cause of sorrow strikes both the rich and the poor. It comprises a test or atonement and a law for all. It is a consolation, however, to be able to communicate with your friends through the means available to you, while awaiting other ways that are more direct and accessible to your senses.*

It is very sad to lose a beloved one. This is, however, a common experience among all people. Every person goes through this, sooner or later. But Spiritism brings us consolation for this unavoidable suffering: it shows us the possibility of communication between the living and the dead. Those who were gone before us are delighted when we remember them. When hearing from them, we become comforted and happy to be in touch with them. By this communication with the spirits, our discarnate beloved ones help and inspire us, showing they are still alive and reminding us that, one day, we will gather again.

The Spirits' Book advises us: we shall not be desperate or unhappy for those who are gone. Sweet memories and longing are good to our beloved discarnates, but pain and despair make them suffer and become afflicted.

Kardec interestingly compares: Let's imagine that two friends, who are really fond of each other, are serving time in the same prison. If one of them is released first, should the other one feel sorry for that? Only if they are very selfish. For if we really care about someone we want them to be happy. How can we be sorry for their freedom?

Thus, prison is the material world, where we suffer so much during life. Freedom is the departure to the spiritual world, the end of a grievous mission, an occasion in which people we truly love go to a new and happier stage. Shouldn't we feel happy for them? Especially if we know we can continue to communicate with our loved ones, hearing from them and sharing affection.

Kardec's question: Isn't the lack of sympathy between persons destined to live together also a source of suffering

that is all the more bitter because it poisons their entire existence?

Spirits' answer: *Very bitter, in fact. However, it is usually one of those misfortunes of which you yourselves are the main cause. In the first place, because your laws are at fault do you believe that God obliges you to live with those you dislike? Moreover, in such unions you almost always seek more to satisfy your pride and ambition rather than enjoy the happiness of a mutual affection. Thus, you suffer the natural consequence of your prejudices.*

Spirits admit that there are, very often, innocent victims who genuinely suffer in these unhappy unions. They are people who, in spite of the efforts to get along with their peers, cannot find means to improve the relationship. In these cases, those who cause the sufferings will be considered responsible for that and, in proportion to their evolution, will no longer have the need to go through these situations of agony. Until then, they must have faith in a better future and keep up with their efforts.

Kardec's question: The worry over death is very perplexing to many persons – but why such worry if they have the whole future in front of them?

Spirits' answer: *It is wrong to have such apprehension, but what do you expect? Since early on, they have been persuaded that there is a hell and a heaven, and that they will most likely go to hell, because they have been taught that whatever belongs to the realm of nature is a mortal sin for the soul. Thus, when they grow up, and if they have any reason at all, they can no longer accept such a belief and become atheists or materialist. It is thus that they are led to believe that nothing exists beyond the present life. As for those who persist in their childhood belief, they fear the eternal fire that must burn them without destroying them. But death does not inspire any fear in the righteous, because faith gives them certainty about the future, hope beacons them with a better life, and charity, whose law they have practiced, gives them the assurance that in the world into which they will enter they will not meet anyone whose encounter they must dread.*

Kardec explains that carnal individuals - that is, people affectionate more to material than to spiritual values – consider the satisfaction of their own desires the ultimate happiness. These people concern, all the time, about earthly matters, which cause them a great deal of agony. As they question the future, knowing they will leave on Earth everything that really matters to them, they have a great fear of death.

On the other hand, moral individuals – those who are in a higher level than purely material necessities, when incarnate, still experience a kind of happiness that material individuals do not reach. As they are not guided for their own desires, they are calm and serene. As they practice the goodness, their deceptions and sorrows are transitory and always overcome.

Kardec's question: Do people have the right to take their own life?
Spirits' answer: *No. Only God has that right. Those who voluntarily commit suicide commit a transgression against that law.*
Kardec's question: Is suicide always voluntary?
Spirits' answer: *Insane individuals who kill themselves do not know what they are doing.*

Spirits explain that individuals who work for a useful purpose, according to their natural vocations, bear life's difficulties with patience, always aiming at a lasting and concrete happiness. For them, life is never so heavy to get to the point of thinking about suicide.

Except for insane individuals, who do not know what they do, people who commit suicide (for not having enough courage to bear the sufferings) will find in the after life the double of the sufferings they tried to avoid in life. And all of those who induce someone to commit suicide will be responsible for murder.

In any circumstance, suicide is a reproachable act and has very bad consequences to the spirit that discarnates this way. This spirit remains for a long time in a state of disturbance and often observes, horrified, the decomposition of their own body in the grave. In future incarnations, they may suffer from mutilations and limitations concerned to the way they killed themselves, not to speak of the painful process of reparation they must necessarily undergo.

FUTURE JOYS AND SORROWS

Kardec's question: Why are human beings instinctively horrified of nothingness?
Spirits' answer: *Because nothingness does not exist.*

Before incarnating, we are aware of what exists before birth and after death. When we incarnate, we keep a slight memory of such realities. The fact that life is brief and can come to an end at any moment makes us have an instinctive concern about the future beyond grave.

Kardec's question: At the moment of death, what is the dominant sentiment in most people: doubt, fear or hope?
Spirits' answer: *Doubt for hardhearted skeptics, fear for the guilty and hope for the good.*

The wisdom of the laws of God, which are based on justice and kindness, leads us to conclude that good and bad people have different fates. The future life is consequence of the acts we have practiced; therefore it is our full responsibility to choose what expect us later. It is important to remind, though, that God always gives us second chances (new existences) to fix the mistakes we have made before.

Kardec's question: What does the happiness of good spirits consist of?
Spirits' answer: *In knowing all things; in feeling no hatred, jealousy, envy, ambition or any of the passions that make*

people unhappy. The love that unites them is a source of supreme happiness. They do not experience the needs, sufferings or anxieties of material life. They are happy with the good they do. Moreover, the happiness of spirits is always in proportion to their progress. Actually, only the pure spirits enjoy supreme happiness; however, this does not mean that the others are unhappy. Between the evil ones and the perfected ones, there is an infinity of gradations, in which enjoyments are proportioned to their moral state. Those who are already sufficiently advanced understand the happiness of those who have reached that state before them and they aspire to it, but it is for them a reason for emulation and not jealousy. They know that it depends on them themselves to reach it and they labor to that end, but with the calmness of a pure conscience. They are happy in no longer having to suffer what is endured by evil spirits.

The meaning of happiness is very different to the pure spirits. If happiness for us, incarnates, most of the times means material comfort, to the evolved spirits it means moral comfort. They don't have to bear corporal life sufferings and they know all things. Thus, they apply their intelligence and acquired knowledge in a useful way, helping the progress of other spirits – and this purpose make them very happy.

Kardec's question: What do the sufferings of little-evolved spirits consist of?
Spirits' answer: *They are as varied as the causes that produce them and in proportion to their degree of impurity, in the same way that enjoyments are in proportion to their degree of purity. We can thus sum them up: to covet everything that they lack to be happy, but not being able to obtain it; to see happiness but being unable to attain it; regret, jealousy, rage and despair arising from everything that keeps them from being happy, remorse and an indescribable mental anxiety. They long for all sorts of enjoyments but cannot satisfy them. That is what tortures them.*

Spirits tell us that the worst torture a spirit can experiment is to believe they are condemned to suffer eternally. Kardec adds that each individual will be accountable for its wrongdoings. The spiritist communications has brought us, in a very concrete way, examples of the sorrows and joys ahead us, depending on our choices while incarnate. When we make a good use of a new incarnation we can reduce the time of sorrows and get closer to the state of moral happiness in which the evolved spirits already find themselves.

When we find ourselves in erraticity (the interval between incarnations) it is as if we are in the summit of a mountain. We look back and see our past; if we look ahead we can plan our future to more rapidly reach the end of this journey. For all our life sorrows (all of them, indeed) are transitory.

Kardec's question: Is it necessary to make a profession of faith in Spiritism and to believe in the manifestations in order to ensure our well-being in the next life?
Spirits' answer: *If that were so, then all of those who do not believe in them, or who have not had the opportunity of learning anything about them, would be disinherited, which is absurd. It is goodness that ensures future well-being. Goodness is always goodness, whatever the path that leads to it.*

Believing in Spiritism, as Kardec explains, helps us to improve and speed up our progress, because it makes each person aware of what they will find ahead, it guides us through the right path, it teaches us to bear the sufferings with resignation and patience, and it deviates us from actions that would delay our progress.

This is not, however, the only way that leads to goodness. Goodness is always goodness, and the most important is not the road that leads us to it. The most important is that we get there.

Kardec's question: Do wicked individuals, who during their life did not recognize their wrongs, always recognize them after death?

Spirits' answer: *Yes, they always recognize them and suffer even more because they regret all the evil they did or of which they were the voluntary cause. Nevertheless, repentance is not always immediate. There are spirits who obstinately persist in doing wrong in spite of their sufferings, but sooner or later they will see that they have taken an erroneous path and repentance will follow. It is for their enlightenment that good spirits work, and towards which you yourselves must work.*

Recognizing our faults is always a cause of suffering. Regret is necessary to not aggravate these faults or prolong our state of inferiority. It is important, as well, to always be vigilant. Because even after our repentance, we can once again be dragged into a mischievous way by spirits less evolved than us.

By praying, we can help less evolved spirits to find the straight path. These prayers, however, will only have effect in case they regret for the harm they caused. No one changes all of a sudden because they are dead. We continue to be who we are and only change through reflections and sorrows.

For this reason, we cannot forget that repentance, itself, is not enough; it helps, but it is not sufficient to make amends for the harm we caused or to conduct us to goodness. In order to attain that, it is necessary to atone, which makes us redeem our faults by undergoing the same kind of difficulties we caused to others. We can start working from this moment to repair these faults: the practice of charity and the dedication to the fellow creatures can be very useful instruments for this reparation.

Kardec's question: **Is there a circumscribed place in the universe that is intended for the punishments and pleasures of spirits according to their merits?**
Spirits' answer: *We have already responded to this question. Punishments and joys are inherent to the degree of a spirit's purification. Each spirit carries within itself the source of its own happiness or unhappiness, and since spirits are everywhere, there is no circumscribed or enclosed place for one or the other. As for incarnate spirits,*

the degree of their happiness or unhappiness depends on the evolution of the world they inhabit.

This demonstrates that heaven and hell are not physical places; they are just ideas or states of mind. The same way, the purgatory is a state of imperfect spirits, who goes through reparation until they are completely pure. As Kardec observes, the fact that this purification happens in a variety of incarnations makes us conclude that purgatory is, in fact, the set of trials we undergo during our corporeal life.

Kardec's question: Will the kingdom of goodness ever be realized on Earth?
Spirits' answer: *Goodness will reign on Earth when, among the spirits who come to inhabit it, the good outnumber the evil ones. They will then make love and justice – the source of goodness and of happiness – reign on Earth. It is through moral progress and the practice of the laws of God that humans will attract good spirits to the Earth and repel the evil ones. However, the evil ones will only leave after humans have banished pride and selfishness from this planet.*

Concerning this question, the last one from *The Spirits' Book*, the spirit Saint Louis explains that Humanity transformation is already predicted and it is not distant. This transformation will be accomplished by a new generation of better spirits who will incarnate on Earth.

People of bad character will, little by little, discarnate and will not return. They will go to other worlds, less evolved, where they will perform grievous missions, making efforts for their own progress. At the same time, they will help improving these new worlds, where they will find fellow beings even less evolved than them.

Our planet will be a much happier place, where love and justice will unite the human kind during the great journey in which we all have to be towards perfection and Light.

ABOUT THE AUTHOR

Laura Bergallo writes for the young audience. She has already published nine books and has three more to be released in 2009. She also has a Bachelor's degree in Social Communication and edits scientific publications.

Her book *The Creature* ("A Criatura") won the Adolfo Aizen Prize/2006 by the Brazilian Union of Writers, as the best youth book of 2004/2005.

Her book *Alice in the mirror* ("Alice no espelho") won the Jabuti Prize-2007 in youth category and was selected to be part of the FNLIJ Catalogue of the 44th Bologna Children's Book Fair.

Her book *Operation Wormhole* ("Operação Buraco de Minhoca") – published by DCL, 2008 - has been selected by the Program for More Culture (Programa Mais Cultura) by the Federal Government and National Library of Brazil, to be distributed in libraries and reading points all over the country.

Published books for young readers:

The four corners of the world (Os quatro cantos do mundo) - (for children) – published by Shogun-Arte, 1986 - This book was selected to the 'Youth-Children's Literature Week', promoted by Petrobras and Macaé City Hall (RJ) in 1987.

A Ghost Story – (Uma História de Fantasma) - (spiritist book) - published by LerBem (Spiritism for Children and Youth Collection), 2001 (sold out) – re-edited in 2008 and published by Lachâtre.

The Spirit's Book for Young Adults and Beginners – (O Livrinho dos Espíritos) - (spiritist book), published by LerBem (Spiritism for Children and Youth Collection), 2002 and 2004 (sold out) – re-edited in 2007 and published by Léon Denis. Also released in France, 2008, by Cesak-Paris, under the title of *Le Petit Livre des Esprits.*

The Gospel according to Spiritism for Young Adults and Beginners (O Evangelho Segundo o Espiritismo para o Jovem Leitor) – (spiritist book) – Lachâtre Publisher

A Train to Another (?) World (Um Trem para Outro (?) Mundo) – published by Saraiva (Jabuti Collection), 2002

This book has been selected to the 'Motion Reading Program' ("Programa Leitura em Movimento"), by Petrópolis City Hall (RJ)

There's an elephant in my bedroom (Tem um elefante no meu quarto) - (for children) – published by Franco (Reading for Pleasure Collection), 2003

The Creature (A Criatura) – published by SM (Steamboat Collection), 2005 - This book won the Adolfo Aizen Prize/2006, by the Brazilian Union of Writers, as the best youth book of 2004 and 2005.

Alice in the Mirror (Alice no Espelho) – published by SM (Muriqui Collection), 2006 - This book has won the renowned Jabuti Prize, in the youth category and has been selected to the FNLIJ of the Bologna's Children Book Fair

The Disappearance Camera (A Câmera do Sumiço) - published by DCL, 2007

Books for Adolescents in production:

The witch and the supernerd (A bruxa e o supernerd) – DCL Publisher

Carioquinha – (for children) – Rocco Publisher

Television scripts:

In Pursuit of the Shadow (Em busca da Sombra) – published in the book '13 Magical Scripts', organized by Luiz Carlos Maciel – Booklink Publisher, 2002

LAURA BERGALLO IS A MEMBER OF THE ASSOCIATION OF WRITERS AND ILLUSTRATORS OF YOUTH-CHILDREN LITERATURE (AEILIJ)